Geraldine Goodkitty

Geraldine Goodkitty

The Tale of A Single Mother
Surviving in An Urban Environment

PURPLE HAZE PRESS

by

F. J. Kercher

Geraldine Goodkitty
©2010 Purple Haze Press®
Publisher: Purple Haze Press®
Purple Haze Press Chief Editor: Pela Tomasello

Purple Haze Press books can be ordered through booksellers or by visiting www.PurpleHazePress.com or www.PurpleV.com or by contacting:

Purple Haze Press
2430 Vanderbilt Beach Road, #108
PMB #167
Naples, FL 34109

First Printing, 2010

Library of Congress Control Number: 2010904727

Author profits from the sale of the book will go to animal rescue organizations.

ISBN: 978-1-935183-05-1

1. Spirituality 2. Love 3. Fiction 4. Consciousness Education

Cover Design by: Jeffrey K. Bedrick, www.jeffreykbedrick.com
Additional Artwork Illustrations by: Sai Clementine
Book design and layout by Darlene Swanson • www.van-garde.com

Dedications and Acknowledgements:

Thank you mom for the gift of love. Thank you dad for the gifts of discipline and perseverance. Thank you Bruce for your help with my computer issues.

I am grateful to Jeffrey Bedrick for his expressive cover design, Sai Clementine for her beautiful illustrations, Diana Schaufler and Parker Juergensen for their valuable input, and my friends Linda Glockner and Trisha Hanrahan for their encouragement.

I thank my teachers, both two-legged and four-legged, for sharing their wisdom with me, primarily Master Suma Ching Hai and Jesus the Christ for spiritual inspiration, Ronn Guidi for artistic inspiration, and the wonderful animals that have graced my life and lent their names, personalities, and physical appearance to most of the characters in this novel.

Finally, thank you Vaishali and everyone at Purple Haze Press, for championing an author friendly approach to publishing and enabling me to share my novel with you.

PROLOGUE

It was deeply comforting to be home again. I felt my way through the familiar darkness to the kitchen, tossed my purse on the counter, and gazed through the window at a brilliant night sky. I leaned across the sink and stood on my tiptoes to get a better view of this dazzling expression of God's handiwork. Were human beings truly the jewel in His crown or a huge thorn in His side? Or was it Her, or perhaps His-Her? Who was responsible for this mess of a world anyway, so beautiful, yet so brutal, so painfully incomplete?

I sat down at the kitchen table to calm myself in the quiet dark. Instead, my mind swirled with questions. Why was I so distressed by the fate of a stray cat? What drew me into the night to find her? Was she hit by a car, attacked by another animal, or was she a victim of disease? It was impossible to tell by looking at her.

I leaned back in the chair to pull her tattered collar from my jean pocket. There was no identification on it, but she had been someone's pet. What twists of fate caused her life to change dramatically and intersect with mine?

I knew a stray cat had decided to make her home on the hill behind my house. A neighbor told me. That was remarkable since he lived three houses away. He was a kindly gentleman who was aware of everything that occurred in the neighborhood. His watchful eye was both reassuring and irritating. He always doused me in well-intentioned advice, and he knew exactly what to do about the stray. In fact, she became the topic of conversation over the next several weeks. "Call Animal Control," he insisted. "They'll trap it and take it . . . better than starving to death."

A cat is an intelligent, resourceful creature. I assumed she could survive without human intervention. My first glimpse of her shocked me into giving her food and water until I could find a better solution. The neighbor immediately warned me, "Feed it and it's yours! Let nature take its course . . . too many cats around anyway." How did he know I was feeding her? Was he really that callous, or was I overreacting? After all, she was just an animal. But she could feel hunger, thirst, fear, and pain, just like me. Wasn't that reason enough to help her?

I continued to listen patiently. "It's going to breed and you'll have a dozen cats living up there in no time." Well, he had a point. I had already seen one kitten. Did he know that, too?

Our conversations became less frequent and more strained. Then, the shouting began. "That stray is using my flowerbeds as a cat pan . . . doesn't even bother to cover it up. Take care of the problem or I will!" He was meticulous about his garden, so this was clearly a serious issue. But why was he certain my stray was the culprit? She wouldn't let me near her, and she was probably too frightened to leave the hilltop to disturb his flowerbeds. Besides, cats are clean creatures. They always cover "it" up. At least I hoped they did.

Finally, he escalated to, "That hill should be cleared anyway. Could be a fire hazard, you know." Now I was angry. I had delayed the annual clean up for several reasons, including the cat problem. However, the hilltop was the last bit of wildness in my city life. I loved it and had no intention of clearing it.

My hand touched something on the table. It was a letter from the City, informing me they had received a complaint about "excessive debris" on the hill. How did the situation become so complex? Could any of this have been prevented? Homeless animals! Angry people! They were everywhere these days. What was I supposed to do about all of the troubled creatures on this obviously troubled planet?

This neighborhood drama starring the man down the street, a stray cat, and me was the least of my problems. Everyday life had become quite difficult, personally and professionally. Were these experiences prodding me gently, or not so gently, toward a crossroads? Was this night another small, yet vital piece in the greater puzzle of my life? Was that why I was allowing it to affect me so intensely?

I glanced at the clock on the microwave. It flashed the same four digits in a monotonous, dispirited way, reminding me again to reset it. I guessed it was after midnight. I had no desire to sleep. I remained at the kitchen table, wrapped in darkness, grappling with the same questions over and over until I was exhausted.

There is no adequate explanation for what occurred next. I dropped my head into the circle of my arms, and before the tears dried on my cheeks, I was adrift in the profound world of night dreams, where our minds weave fantastic tales, and we connect with the highest and the lowest that is in us.

Sometime later I woke with a start and realized I was still in the kitchen. A strangely vivid and detailed dream replayed in my mind.

It involved a stray cat with the odd name Geraldine Goodkitty and her three kittens. I wondered at the source of the dream and the significance of that name. Later, I decided to write about each character in the dream in order to probe its meaning. Geraldine's story began to expand and I continued to write.

Life is a mystery. Geraldine and I explored it together. We experienced our deeper intelligence and discovered the highest law, the Law of Love.

Urban Stray

Chapter 1

Geraldine Goodkitty woke abruptly to the sound of night-walking. She had not experienced deep, peaceful sleep since her world turned hostile. She lifted her head, taking several quick breaths to sample the darkness for any hint of danger. The three kittens tucked close to her body stirred, murmuring softly.

"Quiet, little ones!"

Geraldine nuzzled each of them and moved silently to an opening in the jumble of old boxes where she made her den. She paused there to watch and to listen.

A dog moved slowly down the alley with its muzzle buried in an empty wrapper, pushing it along the pavement, and then steadying it with its front paws to lick every scrap of food from the surface. Geraldine studied the dog's movements, noted the small, dull light around its body, and waited patiently for the inner promptings she trusted with her life. The animal tossed the shredded wrapper aside and continued its slow walk, sniffing the pavement, searching for anything to ease its hunger. Geraldine remained motionless until its scent and its sounds faded into the night. Once again she waited for guidance. Her kittens were fully awake, brushing against her body, winding in and out of her legs, their young eyes round with innocence and wonder.

"Beetle! Tiptoe! I will return for you as soon as I can."

"Are we moving again?"

"Yes, Beetle."

"Not again!"

"Keep silent! Stay hidden!"

Geraldine picked Whisper up gently by the scruff of his neck and jumped from her den into the unknown. She surrendered to her intuition, abandoning familiar pathways, probing side streets, and treading fearlessly along a network of neighborhood fences until she felt drawn to one particular backyard. She jumped down into a flowerbed and detected the scent of raccoon. However, she felt no impulse to abandon this place. As she moved cautiously from shadow to shrub along the edge of the yard, the scent gradually disappeared. A flight of stairs led to a patio set against a small hill dotted with trees. She sensed no further danger and climbed upward, gliding through the moonlight to the top of the hill.

The trees protected a dense layer of ivy and blackberry vines wandering freely over the uneven terrain. She searched until she found a pocket in the thick overgrowth that suited her needs perfectly. When she was satisfied the hilltop was free of predators, she entered her new den, and released Whisper onto a bed of soft leaves.

"Remember!" She kept her manner stern but calm. "Silence!" Whisper curled up with complete trust and drifted back to sleep.

Geraldine did not stop to rest. She immediately retraced her steps. Beetle and Tiptoe were wide-awake, waiting for her to return.

"Moth . . ."

"Beetle, you know what is expected of you."

"But Mother, you don't have to carry me anymore. I'm strong enough to come with you now."

"Absolutely not!"

"But, Moth . . ."

"No!"

Geraldine picked up Tiptoe and rushed into the night.

Beetle tried to wait patiently. He listened for any sign of his mother. He only heard night sounds exciting his curiosity. He gazed at the opening in the boxes leading to the outside world and lost himself in deep imaginings. Inside the box was protection. Outside the box was adventure. He reached for the opening impulsively. His claws slid across the cardboard, and he toppled onto his side. He squirmed to his feet and tried again several times, each failure increasing his determination. Beetle was tired of obeying his mother and of being surrounded by his littermates. "I can't go anywhere without her or them," he thought. His heart filled with anger and resentment. He stretched his tiny body beyond its limits, digging his sharp claws into the box, scratching wildly with his hind feet to support his attempt. With a surge of rebellious energy, he dragged himself to the opening, teetered on the rim for one triumphant moment, and plummeted into the darkness.

Geraldine sensed immediately that Beetle was in danger. She quickened her pace and calmly laid Tiptoe next to Whisper.

"Mother!" Tiptoe cried out fearfully. "Has something happened to Beetle?"

Geraldine could shield most of her thoughts and feelings from the other kittens. Tiptoe was different. She was fully sensitized to the vibrations that flow from all living things.

"Quiet, my love. We will all be together soon. I promise."

Although Geraldine heaved with exhaustion, she ignored her fatigue and set out to rescue her firstborn.

Beetle romped joyously through an enchanted world bounded only by his imagination. He galloped in one direction and then another, spinning, jumping, reaching with outstretched paws for insects whirling overhead. He eagerly followed a sound here and a shadow there and strayed a considerable distance from the den.

Suddenly the magic vanished. An uncomfortable feeling spread through his body. Beetle stood motionless, staring straight ahead into the darkness. He sensed that he must get back to the safety of the den, and he was shocked to discover how far he had wandered. He instinctively dove into a clump of bushes and crouched low beneath the thick growth.

A figure gradually took shape in the moonlight. It was Fat Face, the reigning tomcat in the Brotherhood. Beetle had seen him before at a safe distance on an outing with his mother and his littermates. He pestered his mother for days with questions about Fat Face. He received few answers. However, she warned him repeatedly that any encounter with a tomcat could be deadly.

Beetle shivered with terror as Fat Face approached. His physique alone was intimidating. He was tall and powerfully built. He walked deliberately with his head thrust forward and his tail down, eager to challenge or accept the challenge of anything in his path. He was so close that Beetle could see his notched ears, his scarred face, and the enormous cheeks beneath his keen, predatory eyes. He could smell the peculiar scent of his gray, rumpled fur. He could feel the savage energy pulsing from his body, magnifying the power of his threat. For a fleeting moment, Beetle wondered what it would be like to jump from the bushes and confront Fat Face. This time his fear was greater than his curiosity. He crouched even lower and barely breathed.

Fat Face lifted his head and opened his mouth slightly to sift the night air for any scent worthy of his attention. Beetle flattened himself against the earth and wished he had never left the den. A terrifying cry shot through the night, followed by a round of wails and shrieks. The huge tom shifted his focus, scanning the area around him with heightened interest. Beetle sensed the change. He risked another quick look into the darkness and dropped to the ground in horror. "Oh, no," he whimpered. "Now there are two of them!" Fat Face had turned to confront a cat almost his equal in size. In the next moment they were wrapped around one another in a cloud of dust, screeching and howling, engaged in serious combat. Beetle buried his tiny face, convinced he would never see his mother or littermates again.

The battle stopped as suddenly as it had begun. Beetle found the courage to raise his head slowly, still terrified of what he might see. A triumphant Fat Face was trotting in the opposite direction. His challenger had disappeared. Beetle breathed in deeply, breathed out a sigh of relief, and solemnly promised to obey his mother in the future. He waited until the tomcat was totally out of sight, emerged cautiously from his hiding place, and followed the scent of his own trail back to the den. Although he managed to find the familiar pile of boxes, he could see more than one opening and was uncertain which one led to the nest. He was so exhausted they all appeared hopelessly beyond his reach. However, his encounter with Fat Face left him feeling quite vulnerable. Now he was as anxious to get into the den as he had been to get out.

Beetle studied the possibilities, selected a target, and in a final gargantuan effort, scaled the outer wall of the boxes. He felt them shift a couple of times during his climb, but he reached the opening and belly flopped into the nest. He was stunned by the fall and barely recovered his senses when he felt movement all around him. The boxes tumbled and settled into new positions, locking Beetle in darkness. He was too tired to be concerned. He felt safe, and his energy was spent. He curled his body into a tight ball, quite pleased with himself for surviving his first night of freedom, and slept instantly.

Somewhere in the midst of his dreams, Beetle heard his mother's call. He woke, expecting to see her jump into the den and greet him. Suddenly he realized the opening to the den had disappeared, and he was cut off from his mother and the outside world. He panicked and cried out desperately for help.

Geraldine circled the boxes, sniffing and scratching, searching frantically for a way into the maze to retrieve her kitten. She worked feverishly, using Beetle's cries to guide her. And then she heard footsteps. Humans were always nearby. She shared the alley with them and scavenged the same garbage cans and dumpsters to survive. Some were kind; some were brutal. She no longer trusted any of them.

"Danger, Beetle! Humans!"

Geraldine retreated into the shadows to watch and to wait. A man stopped in front of the boxes and began to search through them. Geraldine remained dead still for minutes that seemed like hours. Suddenly, the man kicked at the boxes angrily, scattering them, and totally exposing Beetle. Geraldine tensed her body, preparing to intervene. The man turned away from the small black figure huddled in the rubbish, steadied himself, and shuffled down the alley.

Geraldine sprang into the moonlight and ran toward her kitten. "Mother, I . . ." She cut his cries short by picking him up in her mouth. Instinctively his body went limp, and she carried him through the night to their new home.

Geraldine refused to rest until she reunited her family. She pushed beyond her survival instinct into the dark tunnel of pain and exhaustion and emerged, at last, on the hilltop. She slowed to a cautious walk as she approached the den. Tiptoe and Whisper jumped to their feet to welcome her.

Tiptoe pressed her forehead lovingly against her mother. "We're together again, just as you promised."

"Yes, little one."

Geraldine solemnly placed Beetle next to his littermates and collapsed beside her kittens, encircling them with her long, thin body. She sniffed the air around her and the earth beneath her to absorb the feeling of this new place. She thanked the Great Mother for guiding her to safety, but kept watch until dawn. Geraldine understood life could change in a heartbeat.

Chapter 2

The morning sun filtered through shadowing trees and veiled the hilltop in an ethereal half-light. In the sheltered darkness of her den, Geraldine yawned and stretched, enjoying the sensuous feel of it. Her kittens nuzzled her belly, searching for the scent of their favorite nipples.

Geraldine watched Beetle climb over Whisper and push one oversized paw in Tiptoe's face. He seemed to enjoy tormenting his littermates, especially Tiptoe, who was the smallest and the weakest. Tiptoe stopped nursing to murmur an objection. Whisper was too content to protest. Geraldine gave Beetle a soft, warning cry and a gentle cuff with her paw. He looked up at her, his green eyes sparkling mischievously. She sensed he was trying to decide whether or not to challenge her. This time he obeyed. He settled in where he was and began to nurse. Geraldine was relieved and a little surprised. She had to be strong and consistent with Beetle. She wanted him to be aggressive, but never cruel; daring, but never foolhardy. Sometimes the effort was exhausting.

The kittens finished nursing and began to groom themselves and each other. Whisper flopped onto his side, allowing Tiptoe to lick his neck and face, purring his approval, gently grooming his sister in return. Geraldine occasionally licked one kitten and then another, concentrating her attention on Beetle. He surrendered to the rhythm of his mother's touch as she patiently groomed his back and the area around his tail. He replayed his adventure over and over in his mind, itching to reveal his secret, yet too frightened of his mother's anger to risk the consequences.

"Oh, if she ever guessed!"

"Beetle, I told you not to leave the den. Your disobedience put us all in danger."

He swung his head around and faced his mother, suddenly shamed by the truth. "How did you know?"

"All she had to do was sniff you," answered Whisper nonchalantly. "You smelled different."

Beetle was impatient with himself for missing the obvious. "I know that."

Geraldine continued grooming him. "I sensed the moment you were in danger."

Tiptoe looked up at her mother shyly. "Felines know things before they happen."

"Well, some things," agreed Beetle, recalling his encounter with Fat Face.

"I know lots of things before they happen," insisted Tiptoe, with a boldness that irritated Beetle.

"Oh, sure."

Geraldine intervened. "The Knowing is a gift from the Great Mother. It will always guide you, unless you choose fear instead."

"Will it guide me, too?" asked Whisper, concerned that the Great Mother might have overlooked him.

"You're feline, aren't you?" Beetle answered, taunting his brother.

"Yes, my love, it is your gift, too." Geraldine cuddled Whisper and Beetle. "It is given at different times and in different ways to each of us. However, Tiptoe's gift is exceptional."

"Her?" Beetle jumped to his feet. "But, she's . . . puny!"

Geraldine brushed Tiptoe affectionately. She understood that Beetle was not intentionally cruel. He was genuinely bewildered that his tiny littermate possessed an ability superior to his own. She nuzzled his head softly. "Her size has nothing to do with it. Be patient, my love, your gift will grow."

"Patience," grumbled Beetle.

"Patience is important to your survival, as important as size and strength."

"How?"

Geraldine looked down at him with smiling eyes. "Be patient, my love. Soon you will understand."

Beetle was offended by the merriment he saw in his mother's eyes. "One day," he thought, "I will show all of you!"

Chapter 3

Geraldine uttered a sharp cry to make sure she had the attention of all three kittens. "I want you to remain here while I explore our new surroundings."

"But, Mother . . ." objected Beetle.

"I will signal you when it is safe."

"But Mother . . ."

"I will signal you!"

Beetle scowled. "When I grow up, I want to be just like Fat Face. Nobody tells him what to do!"

Geraldine was horrified. Fat Face was street bred. In her opinion, he had no idea what it meant to be truly feline. They had met in the Circle, a nocturnal gathering of strays and house cats. She was always keenly aware of his presence. He was the dominant tomcat in the Brotherhood. However, the look in his dark, soulless eyes made her feel so uncomfortable, she went out of her way to avoid him.

Geraldine kept her manner strict and uncompromising. "Remember, come out when I signal and not before."

Geraldine left the den and made her way through the dense, green foliage. The morning air was laced with the fragrance of flowers and trees that bloom in springtime. The scent of prey was all around her. She was relieved she still found no sign of raccoons or other predators. She suspected the raccoons chose to den in the trees along a nearby creek that flowed through the city. Nevertheless, there would always be a need for caution. Suddenly, she stopped and looked back. Beetle's round, little face appeared at the opening of the den and then disappeared, as quickly as an apparition. Geraldine sighed wearily and continued to scan her surroundings when a slight movement caught her attention. A brown squirrel emerged from the overgrowth and scampered up a tree trunk. She paused for a moment to observe him.

Geraldine had always found much to admire in these creatures. They were fastidious, clever, and remarkably agile. She had learned to hunt birds and mice, so she did not perceive the squirrel as prey. However, his sudden, highly animated movements made the desire to chase him irresistible. She crouched low, slinking from spot to spot until she reached the foot of the tree. The squirrel froze, blending so well with his surroundings he seemed to disappear. He leaned forward with one paw at his chest, listening intently. Geraldine sank her sharp claws into the tree, feeling the usual surge of excitement as she shimmied up the trunk.

The squirrel responded with a series of clicking sounds, flicked his bushy tail in agitation, and climbed higher. He paused periodically to check on Geraldine's progress, gazing down at her suspiciously. He considered felines highly unpredictable. Some were harmless; some were deadly. He scanned her vibrations and observed the light around her body. This one appeared to be friendly, but she continued to pursue him . . . and there were those stories. He decided that trust could wait and continued his journey through the tree.

Geraldine kept pace with the squirrel until the upper limbs of the tree began to sway under her weight. She finally watched in disappointment as the squirrel disappeared from sight.

Although Geraldine enjoyed the climb, she was always anxious about the descent. It was an intense mental and physical challenge. Few cats touched ground again with their feline pride intact. Some of her friends never climbed trees. They considered it an unnecessary danger. Her mother had warned her: "Climb if you must, but never linger, and never, never look down." She told her about a feline who was so frightened she clung to a tree limb for days, unable to summon the courage to descend.

Recently, Geraldine heard stories in the Circle about felines called Tree Climbers, who were as comfortable spending their time in trees as they were on solid ground. If the stories were true, there was nothing to fear. However, for now her family was her priority, so she would take no unnecessary risks. She promptly made her way to the main trunk and braced herself. She swung her body around, literally hanging by her claws until she got her footing, and backed down the tree.

Geraldine was breathing rapidly by the time she jumped to the ground. She winced at the persistent pain in her right shoulder and stretched out under the tree to rest. The months of prolonged stress and hunger had weakened her body. She automatically searched the beauty around her for anything that might betray her. She sensed movement and scrambled to her feet. A single, white blossom floated gracefully from above. She observed its descent to join the other fallen ones beneath the tree and wondered sadly if she would ever feel safe again.

Geraldine had been born a fourth generation house cat. Her family proudly belonged to a feline group known as Companions. She spent the first weeks of her life with her feline family in the protected environment of a human household. When she was six weeks old, she began a new life as a Companion to a young boy. She mourned the loss of her mother and her littermates, but soon adapted to the affection and attention the little human lavished upon her.

Geraldine could still feel her terror the day she was stuffed into darkness, taken far from her home, and emptied onto the street to fend for herself. She huddled next to a trash bin, immobilized by her fear, until she heard children's voices. She followed the sounds to a schoolyard, listening anxiously, hoping to turn and find the young human she loved so much kneeling beside her.

The voices faded. The children disappeared. Geraldine began her life as an urban stray. The dismal tales her mother told about the fate of Street Dwellers did not prepare her for the pain-filled reality. She scavenged or she starved. She found shelter, never refuge. She clawed and she bled to stay alive. Youth and a healthy body sustained her for a while, but eventually a recurrent respiratory infection sapped her physical strength. Each day became a labor to begin and a relief to end.

Now Geraldine was a mother. Three kittens depended upon her for their survival. Her love for her kittens was unconditional, and that love gave her the strength to continue.

As soon as Geraldine's breathing returned to normal, she trotted to the edge of the hill. She positioned herself behind a mound of ivy so she could discreetly view the patio. The morning sun had just cleared the trees on the hilltop, bathing most of the patio in its warm light. The area was fenced on two sides and bordered at the front by small shrubs. The ivy covering the face of the hill rambled across the cracked cement. Brilliant red roses grew wild on one side of the patio. A medium-sized tree, laden with pink blossoms, provided shade on the opposite side. Geraldine detected no danger. She could no longer resist. She plunged down the hill into the sunshine, rolling luxuriously on the warm cement, savoring the pleasures of the sun and the fragrance of the roses. She paused a moment longer to enjoy the other scents surrounding her and then returned to a meticulous examination of the area. She found nothing to suggest the raccoons made the hilltop or the patio a regular part of their itinerary.

There was an opening in the shrubbery for the steps leading down to the next level. She peeked cautiously around the shrubs. Another patio at the bottom of the stairs was full of objects she had seen humans use in the past. Geraldine was delighted. She concluded the humans spent most of their time in that area. "How perfect!" she thought. She could observe their activities and minimize the risk of an unexpected encounter.

Geraldine felt good about this place. All of her instincts confirmed it was safe for the present. She climbed the hill and cheerfully signaled her kittens to come out. It touched her heart to watch them march from the den one by one. Geraldine was convinced they were the most intelligent, beautiful kittens born that spring.

Beetle charged down the hill in a flash, half running, half tumbling, his sleek, black coat glistening in the sun. He was dark as a moonless night except for a few tufts of white at his throat and his ears. Geraldine was positive he had inherited his father's size and would be a tall, lean, muscular cat.

Whisper and Tiptoe ventured down the hill more slowly. She

suspected that Whisper deliberately held back to give his sister the encouragement he felt she needed. When they finally reached the patio, Beetle was eager to play. Whisper noticed a lovely gold and brown butterfly fluttering from shrub to shrub. He sat perfectly still, entranced by its movement and its beauty. Only the tip of his black, plume-like tail swished from side to side. Beetle seized the opportunity to launch a surprise attack. He jumped sideways several times, the hair on his back and his tail bristling, and broke into a full run. "Watch out!" cried Tiptoe. Whisper immediately flipped onto his back. Beetle pounced on him and Whisper grabbed his brother's neck with his front paws, kicking him repeatedly with his hind feet. The two kittens rolled over and over on the warm cement, growling and snarling.

Tiptoe observed her brothers warily, trying to decide whether to join them. Geraldine could understand her reluctance. Although Beetle and Whisper never hurt each other, their battles certainly looked and sounded ferocious. She whipped her tail from side to side to get Tiptoe's attention, watching her carefully, measuring every response. Tiptoe seemed uninterested, but she did not always respond like her brothers. Almost everything about her had been different from the moment she was born.

Geraldine thought the birthing process was complete when a tiny sac, as fragile as a teardrop, slipped unexpectedly from her body. She gently cleaned the shriveled, undersized kitten, anxiously waiting for any sign of sound or movement. Her concern soon vanished. This kitten's body was weak, but her spirit was strong.

In some ways, Tiptoe was Geraldine's mirror image. She had inherited her short, thick, silver and black coat with its exotic patterns of stripes and spots, a serene, genteel face with the same distinctive scarab marking on her forehead, and green eyes glistening with light that were rimmed in black. However, Tiptoe's eyes were so large they dominated her tiny, heart-shaped face, and her silver and black whiskers all curved downward. Her tail was exceptionally long, and despite her timid nature, she always carried it high over her upper back with a slight curl. Geraldine knew it would be the envy of every feline in the Circle. Her long, sliver of a body rested on hind legs so much longer than her front legs, that she appeared to be walking on the tips of her toes.

Tiptoe idly pawed at her mother's tail, but her attention wandered from the earth to the treetops.

"Mother, tell me about the Tree Climbers."

"I only know what I have heard in the Circle."

Tiptoe tucked her legs comfortably under her body. "Tell me!"

"Well, Tree Climbers spend a part of each day way up there." Geraldine indicated the upper branches of a large tree on the hill.

Tiptoe looked up in awe at the majestic presence that seemed to connect with the sky.

"Why?"

"I'm not certain."

"Tell me more."

"Some felines consider them wise. Some consider them fools."

"What do you think?"

"I have never met a Tree Climber, so I have no opinion. Apparently, they do tell fascinating stories about our past."

"What kinds of stories?"

"Well, they insist that there was a time when humans revered us above all other creatures."

"Really?"

"But there was another time when they despised our kind and tried to destroy us."

"Why?"

"I don't know, little one."

"Will I ever meet a Tree Climber?"

"Maybe one day. My friend Tosey told me they sometimes visit the Circle."

"Will you take me to the Circle?"

"Of course."

"Soon?"

"You must be older."

"How much older?" Tiptoe asked impatiently.

"You must trust me to make that decision."

Beetle squealed, distracting both of them. Whisper had finally taken the offensive. "At last!" thought Geraldine. His patience seemed endless, but Beetle was relentless. Whisper danced beside his brother for a moment and then attacked, wrapping his front legs around Beetle's neck, biting him on his head and shoulders. Beetle was surprised and delighted. He enjoyed their games far more when Whisper lost his patience and fought back in earnest.

Geraldine was amazed at the variety of sounds Beetle used to intimidate his brother. He had already developed an extensive threat vocabulary. However, she had never heard Whisper utter a shriek or a cry. All of the sounds he made were barely audible. Sometimes he opened his mouth and produced no sound at all. She was concerned. It was important for him to develop an adequate vocabulary to support his natural, telepathic abilities. Geraldine recalled sitting beside her mother, attentive and eager to learn. "Remember, little one," her mother had advised her, "observe similarities, observe differences. Simply observe."

Geraldine knew she must watch her feelings for Whisper. She was determined to love her kittens equally. As he matured, he clutched at her heart in a special way. He looked just like his father, Romeo. He had the same long, white, silky coat with random splashes of black, the same gold eyes edged in black, the same gentle strength.

The thought of Romeo filled Geraldine with melancholy. She refocused her attention on her kittens. They could brighten her spirit during the worst of times. Suddenly, she realized how soon they would take their place in the world, and her melancholy deepened. Her reaction puzzled her. She had always known they would leave her some day. She devoted herself to preparing them to survive successfully on their own. "But what will their futures be?" she wondered. "Are my little ones destined to become Street Dwellers?"

It was common knowledge in the Circle that the life of a Street Dweller could be short and painful. Geraldine had even heard stories of some who were held captive by humans and subjected to incredible horrors. Could these things happen to her kittens? How often her mother had counseled her: "Accept what is, my love, do your best, and trust in the Great Mother." She took comfort in these memories. Yet, her mother's advice seemed to belong to a different world. Life on the streets had challenged almost everything her mother taught her.

Geraldine refused to allow fear to infect such a splendid day. She joined her family at play and then relaxed in the healing warmth of the sun until it moved away from the patio. When she signaled her kittens to return to the hilltop, they obeyed without a single protest.

The kittens played for hours near the den under their mother's watchful eye, chasing one another wildly through the ivy, caught up in an endless cycle of hiding, attacking, and retreating. At dusk, they followed her into the den, eager to curl up in her warm embrace. Geraldine was pleased to see them tired. They had little opportunity for exercise while they lived in the alley.

"I want to stay here," Beetle informed his mother.

"We are safe, at least for now. There are humans nearby, and we must still be cautious. Fortunately, in some ways humans and felines are alike."

Beetle found this hard to believe. "How?"

"Routine is comforting to them. I will observe their daily activities, explore a little further, and then make a final decision."

"Why don't you like humans anymore?" asked Whisper.

"I don't dislike them. I loved my human family and enjoyed the comfort of the surroundings they provided."

Tiptoe stretched her tiny body. "Mother likes humans. She just doesn't trust them. She told us how wonderful it felt to sit with the little human and feel him stroke her fur."

Geraldine's mind wandered back to the moments she treasured, to the touch of the little human's hand and sound of his voice as he spoke to her softly. She did not understand all of the words. Only the few she heard often were familiar and had meaning, "Geraldine . . . good kitty . . . love . . ."

"I would like that too," agreed Whisper.

"Well, not me!" Beetle sat up and glared at his brother indignantly. "We give up a lot for all that comfort."

"What do you mean?" asked Tiptoe.

"Don't you understand anything? We give up our freedom. Humans tell us when to eat, what to eat, when to stay in, when to go out. After we finally adjust to their silly routine, they send us away for no reason at all! Right, Mother?"

Geraldine looked at Beetle sadly, searching her heart for a response. "We have to compromise whenever we share our life with another creature. We give up some things and get others. But, totally lose our freedom? Live like the canine? Certainly not! We felines are far too clever. I let my humans know when I wanted to leave and return. If I did not like the food, I simply refused to eat it. If you are persistent, they will change the food."

Beetle eyed his mother skeptically. "Why did they send you away?"

"I'm not sure. The mother human must have felt she had good reason. She was never cruel. Like most of her kind, she was just . . . careless."

Beetle stared at his mother defiantly. "And who suffers when they are careless?"

"But," Whisper asked hopefully, "all humans are not alike, are they, Mother?"

"No more than all felines are alike. Some are like the little human. He was always gentle and affectionate toward me. He would never have sent me away. Others treat felines with total disrespect."

"Why?"

"Maybe because we look different and don't make the same sounds they do. I guess they assume we have no thoughts, no feelings, and therefore, no value."

Beetle stood and declared boldly, "A feline is more important than any human!"

Geraldine pressed her chin affectionately against his tiny forehead. "My own mother taught me that no creature is more important than another. Some are bigger. Some are smaller. All play a significant role in what is."

Beetle took a few moments to digest this information and continued on. "Why would any feline want to associate with humans?"

"Actually, humans encouraged us to stay with them. They discovered that we could be useful. They consider one of our favorite prey their enemy."

"Does everything have to be useful?" Whisper asked.

"Everything that exists has a purpose."

Beetle licked his coat vigorously. "I've got it! If we serve their purpose, humans keep us around. If we don't, they toss us out."

Geraldine tried to explain, "That's not always . . . "

Beetle interrupted, "I will serve *my* purpose!"

"My mother was a Companion and succeeded in doing both," Geraldine pointed out. "You have an advantage. We were given to human families. You can choose."

"Why would I? I don't need them for anything."

Geraldine thought for a moment. "There are many reasons— affection, comfort, stability."

"Will you ever trust humans again?" asked Tiptoe.

"I was born a Companion. My mother and her mother before her, into the time we cannot remember, were Companions. I would have tried to find another human family . . . " Geraldine stopped and then continued quickly. "Soon you will each have to decide what direction you want your life to take. Remember, my loves, all humans are not cruel, but make them prove themselves before you trust them."

"I'm the only one I'm going to trust!" Beetle vowed.

Geraldine suddenly felt very tired. "Little ones, it is time to rest."

The kittens sensed their mother's fatigue. They did not engage in their usual disagreement over sleeping positions. They each made a pillow of her thick, plush fur and settled in for the night. Geraldine cleaned her kittens meticulously, drawing comfort from the sound of their contented purrs. When she finished grooming Beetle, he looked at her with eyes reflecting a hint of apology.

"Mother, I know I can trust you."

"Always, my love."

Eventually, Geraldine fell into a light, fitful sleep. A wound from the past surfaced to torment her dreams. She pawed at the sides of an imaginary prison, pleading with soft-voiced cries for her mother's help. Her muscles jerked and her sides heaved as she struggled for each new breath. An alien scent plunged her into darkness— twisting, squirming, rocking, careening, her mother and her little human slipping farther and farther away. Her feelings of terror and loss threatened to overwhelm every level of her being when she woke suddenly.

Tiptoe gave her a drowsy look. "Mother, you are dreaming again."

Geraldine was concerned she had frightened her kittens. "There is nothing to fear, little ones. You are safe."

Tiptoe was already sound asleep. Whisper and Beetle still

breathed quietly. It eased her troubled heart to realize that her kittens experienced the tranquil sleep of the innocent she had known so long ago. She wondered if it was possible to recover what she had lost.

Geraldine tried to relax. Her ears shot forward at the slightest sound. She was also hungry, but she chose to remain with her kittens and hunt in the early morning.

Chapter 4

The kittens still slept peacefully when Geraldine slipped away at dawn. Prey was easier to find than to catch, but she finally enjoyed her first full meal in a couple of days. She felt nauseated after eating and calmed her stomach with some tender shoots of green grass.

Geraldine also needed a reliable source of water. She snuck down the stairs for a quick look at the lower patio and discovered the welcome scent of water and the disturbing scent of raccoon. She slinked toward a birdbath, rising up on her hind legs to lap greedily from the basin. She caught more scent that she recognized from a large barrel and jumped onto the edge to investigate.

The barrel not only contained water, but a variety of plants and small fish. She knew from previous experience that the taste of this water would be far more to her liking than the contents of the birdbath. As she lapped the water with great satisfaction, the spirited movement of the fish captured her attention. She had only seen this kind of creature on one other occasion. She watched the fish with tense excitement, and her heart struggled with unwelcome memories.

Geraldine suddenly jumped to the ground and hid in the shrubbery. The back door opened and a woman came down the stairs carrying a bag that she deposited in a garbage can. Geraldine shuddered at the sight and hoped she would never be forced to scavenge again. She watched the human place several small objects on the fence in a neat row and reenter her house. While she waited to hear the back door close and lock, she saw the squirrel scamper toward the objects on the fence and eagerly consume them. In the next instant he was gone. "How interesting," she thought.

Geraldine remained hidden a few minutes longer and then proceeded to examine every object on the patio, searching out any potential danger. Her next task was to explore the world beyond the backyard. She was frightened whenever she ventured into the unknown. The responsibilities of motherhood and her own intense curiosity pushed her beyond her more timid self.

Geraldine jumped from the garden gate and scurried down the driveway, staying as close to the hedge as possible. She stopped periodically to sniff it thoroughly. It was covered with scent, but none that she recognized. She was no more than two blocks from her old territory, yet the environment was quite different. She could hear the sounds of life all around her without the din of heavy traffic. There were more trees, shrubs, and colorful flowers wherever she looked.

Geraldine moved carefully from house to house, cloaking herself with growing things whenever possible. She stopped at the end of the block to decide whether or not to continue and noticed a large, strange looking cat reclining in an open window, her huge bulk pressing against the screen. She walked down the driveway to get the cat's attention. She stretched out comfortably and they scrutinized each other until they were both at ease. Geraldine finally extended a friendly greeting.

"Isn't it a beautiful morning?"

"Out there? I don't think so!"

"Don't you enjoy spending time out here?"

"Occasionally I leave my den, but I am carried wherever I go."

Geraldine was amazed. "Don't you miss the pleasurable feel of the earth beneath your feet or the freedom to wander from place to place?"

"Wander? Out there?" Her new acquaintance was incredulous. "Catch parasites? Dirty my feet? Soil my fur? You can't be serious! My humans take pride in my luxurious coat. They groom me daily, and that gives me great pleasure. I purr, and that gives them great pleasure."

Geraldine scrutinized the mass of thick fur disapprovingly. This feline was obviously incapable of grooming herself.

The cat in the window retaliated with a haughty look. "My humans call me Gorgeous. Many of their kind come from far away just to admire me."

Sometimes Geraldine found it difficult to appreciate the human sense of beauty. She could not imagine why they considered this cat beautiful. Her appearance violated every rule of feline aesthetics. Her head was large and flat looking. Her ears were small. The highly prized line of the head, neck, and body was completely obscured by a profusion of thick, dark gray hair with an odd blue cast. Her large, round eyes were the only discernable feature on her face, and they were orange. "Most unusual," thought Geraldine.

Geraldine wanted to know more about Gorgeous and the way she lived. "Tell me, if you never like to be out here, what do you do in there?"

"What is expected of me, of course."

Geraldine did not understand. Gorgeous continued.

"I sit."

Geraldine waited. "Yes . . . "

"I lay."

"What else?"

"I sleep."

"That's all?"

"I eat, but only what pleases my taste."

Geraldine waited to hear more, but Gorgeous did not continue.

"And?"

"Occasionally I mate."

"That's all?"

"You seem surprised."

"Well . . . yes . . . how else do you spend your time?"

"I try to amuse myself, but there are many restrictions here." She sighed, "It is better to do nothing."

"Nothing?" Geraldine tried to imagine such a life.

"Great beauty can be a burden, you know. Come by again," urged Gorgeous, before Geraldine could ask any more questions. "Your company pleases me." She lowered her large head to a mound of gray hair where her legs should be and apparently went to sleep.

Geraldine decided to accept her invitation. She was still curious about Gorgeous and her lifestyle. Gorgeous seemed quite content with her situation. Geraldine had experienced the pleasure of lying in a screened window, enjoying the sun and an occasional breeze. She was not certain she would want to totally surrender her freedom to touch the earth and to surround herself with fresh air, flowers, and sunshine.

Geraldine had seen all that was necessary in the neighborhood for now. She noted which humans kept canines as pets and which did not. She would explore further on another day.

When Geraldine returned to the den, the kittens questioned her about every detail of her journey. They were especially eager to know whether or not this would be their new home.

"I am still not certain, little ones. Be patient. Soon I will be able to decide. I discovered the scent of the creature with the black eyes near the human's den."

"Oh!" Tiptoe was obviously upset.

"I found no evidence of its presence anywhere near us. If we are prudent, there is no reason for our paths to cross. Do you understand?"

All three kittens nodded gravely.

Chapter 5

Geraldine monitored the woman's activity during the following week and found her quite predictable. She decided it was safe in the morning just after first light to slip down the stairs to the lower patio for a drink of water. Night creatures like the raccoon were generally on their way back to their dens, and she had observed no human activity in or around the house that early. As she lapped water from the barrel, she felt she was being watched. She glanced around quickly and saw the woman staring at her through a large window. She hid immediately and returned to the hilltop through a neighboring yard. She kept her kittens in the den for the rest of the day.

"Isn't there some place we can go where we don't have to hide?" asked Whisper.

Geraldine had no answer.

Beetle gave his mother a grumpy look. "Fat Face doesn't hide."

Geraldine's eyes glowed with light. "Even Fat Face knows there are times when it is prudent to blend with your surroundings."

"I saw him fight. He didn't hide."

"Maybe not from other felines. But what about humans and canines?" asked Whisper.

"And those scary creatures with the huge claws and big black eyes," added Tiptoe with a shudder.

"You will learn when to fight and when to withdraw," Geraldine assured them. "The Knowing will guide you."

Whisper looked at his mother with deep affection and respect. "Mother kept us safe from the canine."

"Yes. And then what happened?" Beetle stormed at his brother. "We found another place to hide!"

Geraldine rubbed her cheek against his soft fur. "I wish there was a place where we could enjoy all of the beauties of our life without the danger."

"Do we have to move?" Whisper asked.

"I don't think so. There is no reason for the human to suspect that we make our home here. We are well hidden. However, we must always be ready for change." She drew closer to her kittens to comfort them. "Don't be concerned. Rest now."

Geraldine cradled her kittens in the curve of her body, and they soon forgot the perils of the outside world. They trusted in their mother's love and her total commitment. They knew she would give her life to protect them.

Early the next morning Geraldine heard the woman open her back door right on schedule and go into the backyard to tend to her plants. However, a few minutes later she heard her walk up the stairs to the upper patio. Geraldine jumped to her feet. Her body stiffened. She listened tensely to sounds that seemed familiar, but were difficult to interpret.

"Oh, no," moaned Beetle, certain they would have to move again.

"Quiet!" ordered Geraldine. She did not relax until she heard the woman close the back door and lock it. "There it is— the final sound. She is back in her den."

"What happened, Mother?" asked Whisper.

"The human was at the bottom of the hill," answered Tiptoe.

"What was she doing?"

"She . . ."

Geraldine interrupted Tiptoe. "Rest, my loves. I will return shortly." She added firmly, "Do not leave the den!"

As Geraldine slinked to the edge of the hill, she noticed the squirrel moving effortlessly through the trees. She had to admit he almost equaled a feline in the quick, efficient beauty of his movements. He sensed Geraldine's presence and sat up straight with both paws at his chest. He seemed curious about her this morning. She glanced down at the upper patio and saw two large objects in front of the shrubbery near the stairs. She quickly looked back at the squirrel. He merely gave her a satisfied look and continued his journey through the trees.

Geraldine climbed down the hill cautiously. She hesitated at the bottom to make sure no human was near and moved toward the objects slowly. She could hardly believe the information her senses provided. She discovered two dishes, one filled with food and the other with water. She knew the human had no pets. Street Dwellers and Companions had warned her in the Circle about traps with food as the lure, but she found no evidence of a trap. For a moment she felt the food and water might have been left for her. She promptly dismissed this idea because of her more recent experience with humans.

Finally, Geraldine decided to simply embrace her good fortune. She rushed to the dishes, eagerly consuming the food and lapping the water, pausing every few seconds to watch for intruders. As soon as she finished her meal, she munched green grass to ease another bout with nausea, groomed herself, and hurried back to her kittens. The kittens were anxious to learn what their mother had discovered.

"Little ones, there was food and water at the bottom of the hill."

Whisper sat up straight and alert. "Maybe the human has felines . . . maybe even canines!"

"No," Geraldine assured him, "I am certain she does not. I thought it might be a trap. Remember, always be aware of that possibility."

"How will we know?"

"There are ways. I will teach you."

"Then who put the food there, and why?" asked Beetle.

"The human did," answered Tiptoe. "She put the food there for us." Her eyes sparkled with innocent enthusiasm. "Maybe the human is a gift from the Great Mother."

"Are you serious?" Beetle turned his back on his sister and buried his face in his mother's fur.

"Mother . . .?" Tiptoe looked to her mother for support.

"Well, perhaps," she answered calmly. She wanted to believe the woman could be their friend. Her past experience remained a potent reminder to move slowly. The safety of her family depended upon it.

Beetle lifted his head suddenly and looked straight into his mother's eyes, demanding an answer. "And why isn't there a Great Father?"

"Some felines believe there is. Most agree the Great Feline exists. Some claim to see its image in the High Place."

Tiptoe rushed to the opening of the den to gaze at the sky.

"Not yet, my love. My mother told me it is only possible to see the Great Feline when the High Place is dark."

Beetle was skeptical. "Have you seen it?"

"No."

"How do we know this Great Feline even exists?"

"It is a mystery, my love, but we know."

That evening Geraldine heard the woman move around the backyard as usual and climb the stairs to the upper patio to refill the dishes. The woman reentered her house and Geraldine heard the final sound. She charged down the hill to the patio, but resisted the impulse to begin eating. She peeked through the shrubs, waiting patiently until she was absolutely certain the woman would not return.

Geraldine gobbled down her second meal in one day, groomed herself, and felt optimistic again. She had forgotten how wonderful it felt to be full. She rejoined her kittens immediately to give them the good news. All three of them mewed happily. They loved the environment on the hilltop and were thrilled that it might be their permanent home.

As Geraldine and her kittens lay comfortably together, secure in one another's presence, she was startled once again by sounds from the upper patio. She jumped to her feet and left the den immediately to investigate. However, the woman had merely returned to remove the empty dishes. Geraldine went back to the den promptly to reassure her kittens. She drew them close to her and soon the entire family was lost in their dreams.

Sometime, deep in the night, Geraldine felt Tiptoe slip away from her. She did not try to stop her. She was more curious than fearful about what she might do. Tiptoe reclined at the opening of the den and stared up at the night sky. She was searching for the image of the Great Feline.

Chapter 6

Geraldine continued to find food and water on the upper patio every morning and every evening. She emptied both dishes and the woman removed them after dark. Nothing remained to attract raccoons or other intruders. Nevertheless, Geraldine searched the hilltop and the patio diligently each day for any indication of trespassers. She was also careful to vary her route when she left or returned to her den. She took all of the daily precautions necessary to protect the location of her new home.

Geraldine discovered there was only one day of the week when the woman's movement around the house and yard was unpredictable. The information she gathered with her exquisite feline senses, her intelligence, and her deep inner knowing convinced her at last that it was safe to remain on the hilltop.

There was little sunshine on the hill, so whenever it was possible Geraldine allowed her kittens to accompany her down to the patio to play. She never permitted them on the patio until she had finished her meals. She wanted to teach them to hunt before they tasted the food the human supplied.

"Are we really going to stay?" Tiptoe asked, as she wiled away an afternoon in the sunshine.

Geraldine stretched out under the tree, as content as she had been in months. "I am as certain as I can be."

A gentle rain had passed during the night, cleansing the hilltop and the patio. It sweetened the air, adorning the trees and plants with iridescent droplets glittering rainbow colors in the sunlight. Tiptoe relaxed with her paws tucked under her chin. Whisper played in the thicket near the wild roses. Beetle eagerly pursued any insect that crawled or flew across his path.

"Oh, Mother," cried Tiptoe, purring and stretching happily. "I wish we could stay this way forever!"

"So do I, little one. But nothing stays the same— forever."

"Why?"

"Life is change."

"Why?"

"All things grow, or they perish. Change is part of the growing."

Geraldine saw the happiness suddenly vanish from Tiptoe's tiny face. "Don't let fear about the future spoil your happiness today."

Tiptoe's expression did not change.

Geraldine tried another approach. "Just let the future unfold, little one, and be grateful for the gifts the Great Mother is sharing with you."

There was a hint of reproach in Tiptoe's gentle, trusting eyes. "Is that what you do, Mother?"

Geraldine groomed herself to hide her embarrassment. She realized she was giving advice she sometimes did not follow. "Not always," she admitted. "But my life is better when I do. It is good advice given to me by my own mother."

"How much longer will we be together?" asked Tiptoe.

"We still have plenty of time. One day you will be ready to make a life of your own. In fact, you will be eager to do so."

"That's for sure!" agreed Beetle.

"Won't you miss us just a little?" Tiptoe asked her brother.

Beetle was positive that he would not, but even he could not ignore the deep affection he saw in her large, sensitive eyes. "Well, a little . . . but as Mother explained, nothing stays the same."

Tiptoe knew her mother must be right. She was surrounded with warm sunlight, yet her slender body shivered with cold. She tried hard, but she could not imagine life without her mother and her brothers.

A loud squawking sound disrupted the peaceful quiet of the patio. Whisper ran from the thicket with a mockingbird in hot pursuit. It flew low over Whisper and swooped down on Beetle, pecking him at the base of his tail. It then flew back to join its mate perched on the fence. The bird continued to taunt them from a safe distance. Beetle was beside himself with indignation.

"Canine brain! We eat your kind!"

The birds appeared unimpressed, squawking and brazenly dancing along the fence. Beetle was outraged.

Geraldine tried to calm him. "There is no reason for anger. They must have young nearby. They defend their little ones just as I would defend you."

"You didn't tell me they attack us."

"I did tell you to always be prepared for the unexpected."

"'A feline must be flexible in both body and mind to survive.'" Whisper repeated his mother's instruction exactly as she had originally given it.

Beetle gave his brother a malevolent look.

The incessant squawking finally heightened the tension to an unbearable level.

"Such noisy, irritating creatures," thought Geraldine. "Return to the den," she ordered her kittens. Whisper and Tiptoe obeyed. Beetle did not move.

The female flew just above Geraldine's head to distract her while the male swooped down to peck at Beetle a second time. Geraldine chased them back to their perch on the fence. Once again she instructed Beetle to go back to the den. But, the more the birds taunted him, the more determined Beetle was to avenge himself. He crouched low, swishing his tail from side to side, glaring at the birds.

"There is a time to fight and a time to walk away. Learn to know the difference, little one."

Beetle still did not move.

"Never waste your energy. It is far too precious."

Beetle ignored his mother and crept toward the fence. Geraldine lost patience. She picked him up by the scruff of his neck and carried him up the hill.

Chapter 7

The kittens were eager to explore every inch of their surroundings. Geraldine found it increasingly difficult to restrain their will to experience. They wanted to participate in all of her activities. Every day they pestered her to take them down to the patio to eat with her.

"What does the food taste like?" Beetle asked, full of his usual curiosity.

"It is . . . acceptable," answered Geraldine.

"Is it more pleasing to the taste than the prey you bring home to us?" asked Whisper, who possessed the most discriminating palate of the three kittens.

Geraldine was careful not to stimulate his curiosity. Whisper had inherited his father's conformation, coloring, and his love for food.

"It is acceptable," she repeated, deliberately noncommittal.

Geraldine began life on the streets without the ability to hunt efficiently. Since she had lived indoors from birth until she was abandoned, she never had the opportunity to acquire sound hunting skills. Fortunately, she met her friend Tosey, observed her, and learned to hunt by trial and error. Meanwhile she nearly starved to death.

Now Geraldine faced the grim possibility that her kittens might also become Street Dwellers. She wanted them to master the hunt before they savored the pleasures of food conveniently provided by humans. Good skills would increase their chance of survival. She had already brought dead prey to the den to teach them what to hunt. Soon she would bring them live prey to teach them to kill properly and to eat what they kill.

Beetle persisted. "So when can we taste it for ourselves?"

"Can we go with you next time?" asked Whisper.

Tiptoe wanted to be sure she would also be included. "I want to go, too!"

"Patience, little ones. There is something else I want you to experience first."

"What?" asked Whisper, delighted by the prospect of learning something new.

"The hunt, my loves."

The kittens were impressed for the moment. However, the next morning they began again, cajoling and pleading. All three of them pestered Geraldine mercilessly. She finally relented. "All right. You can come with me now. Follow me closely and don't make a sound."

The kittens lined up behind her quietly and obediently followed her down the hill. The moment their paws touched the patio they charged toward the food dish. It was too small for all of them to eat at once so a conflict developed immediately. Tiptoe tried various ways to get to the food, running from one side to the other, ducking under her brothers, pushing between them, crawling over them.

Geraldine finally drove all three of them away from the dish and made them wait for her to eat first. However, her lesson in restraint seemed lost on them. They had ravenous appetites and stormed the dish once again, pushing, shoving, and snarling at one another. They managed to get their feet in the food and to overturn the water.

Geraldine was a patient teacher, but she wondered if her kittens would ever learn proper feline manners. She decided it was fortunate she was not as hungry as usual. They compensated for her lack of appetite and devoured every morsel. She herded them back to the den, convinced she had made a mistake.

After a meticulous grooming session, the kittens curled up beside Geraldine and began to doze. The sound of their loud, monotone purrs had a tranquilizing effect upon her and she slowly began to drift.

Images from the past and the present floated through her mind in a jumbled, dreamlike manner. One image, with all of its pleasure and its pain, returned again and again to haunt her. It was the vision of a splendid white and black feline with slanted gold eyes rimmed in black, and gorgeous white brows and whiskers.

Tiptoe saw her mother's thoughts and felt her feelings. "Where is Father?" she asked.

Geraldine was still lost in her reverie.

"Why isn't Father with us?"

The question startled Geraldine. She took a moment to compose herself. "He brought me to his human family several times. They didn't accept me."

"Why?"

"Either they couldn't or they wouldn't."

"Why didn't he leave them and go with you?"

"It is not the feline way, my love."

"Does he know about us?"

"No."

"Does he know where you are?"

"No."

"But you miss him and we miss him."

"For now, little one, my place is with you and his place is with his human family."

"Will we ever see him?"

"Possibly . . . one day . . . when you are a little bit older."

"How much older?"

"You must trust me to make that decision."

"Mother, I trust you, but waiting takes so long."

"Patience, little one."

"Tell me more about him."

"What would you like to know?"

"He looks like Whisper, doesn't he?"

"Why, yes."

Whisper was half listening, half dozing. "Really? Father looks like me?"

"Yes, little one."

"Are Father and Whisper alike in other ways?" asked Tiptoe.

Beetle scowled. "I hope not."

"My loves, your father is strong. He is also sensitive and gentle."

Whisper was now wide-awake and interested. "I want to be just like him."

"You would!" Beetle nipped at his brother lightly. "He sounds weak to me."

Whisper was angry. "You never know when to keep your thoughts to yourself or to change them for better ones."

"Beetle, my love, your father never picked a fight, but he never lost one either. You are confusing gentleness with weakness."

"Mother, I understand." Tiptoe asserted confidently, "The weak are afraid to be gentle."

Beetle lunged at Tiptoe. "The weak are gentle because they are afraid of the strong."

Tiptoe cringed and moved closer to her mother. Whisper rose to his haunches, ready to defend his sister.

"Calm yourselves! Both can be true, my loves. But the gentleness in your father comes from his heart."

Beetle recalled the fight between Fat Face and his adversary. Geraldine saw the pictures in his mind. She continued. "The feline way is to engage an opponent mentally. If a feline fights smart, the opponent will normally yield. Your father fights smart."

Geraldine could feel Beetle resist her explanation. "A true feline only attacks his opponent physically as a last resort."

"Well, I want to be strong like Fat Face and be in the Brotherhood."

Geraldine stared deep into Beetle's intense, little eyes and glimpsed a future that broke her heart; a brutal existence filled with violence, hunger, and disease. "There is more to living than the Brotherhood."

"Like what?"

"Stability, companionship . . . love."

"For Companions maybe, but not for Street Dwellers."

"We don't have to be Street Dwellers," suggested Whisper.

"I do," argued Beetle. "I want to be free!"

"My love, there was once freedom in the Old Way. Human contact changed that. Neither Street Dwellers nor Companions will know that kind of freedom again." Geraldine wondered how she could make Beetle understand. She began slowly, "Beetle, your father is a Companion."

"My father . . . a Companion!" Beetle found this difficult to accept.

"Your father is idolized by his humans. They provide for him out of the deepest affection."

"Ugh," groaned Beetle. "Does he do anything for himself?"

"Certainly!" exclaimed Geraldine with amusement. "He is quite capable, I assure you. He . . ."

"My father . . . a Companion," repeated Beetle.

"Listen to Mother for a change," ordered Whisper with a deep, loud, sustained growl.

Geraldine, Beetle, and Tiptoe were astonished by the strange sound he uttered.

"More canine than feline," thought Geraldine. "Well, it was a sound, and we all heard it."

Whisper was equally surprised by the intensity of his response. "Mother," he continued gently, "I want to know more about Father and the life he leads."

"It is true that your father's freedom is restricted. His humans allow him to roam when it is light, but never in darkness. However, he is gifted with intelligence as well as beauty. He manages to outsmart his humans when he wants to. He loves his way of life and considers the restrictions acceptable."

Beetle was adamant. "I want to be like Fat Face. I want to be free."

"We must learn to distinguish between what we want and what we need. There is a difference. We must understand this in order to make sound choices for ourselves."

"Well, I will never be a Street Dweller!" Tiptoe announced with deep conviction. "I am going to be a Tree Climber!"

"Little one, I thought you wanted to be a Companion."

"I will be both."

"I don't know if that is possible."

"Why?"

"Tree Climbers live according to the Old Way."

"What does that mean?"

"They live a solitary life . . . mostly away from humans."

"But I want to be wise."

"Wisdom never comes easily, my love. Few felines value it."

"I don't care!" replied Tiptoe boldly. "I am going to be a Tree Climber and a Companion."

"Do Tree Climbers have a special place in the Circle?" asked Beetle.

"No, little one. All are equal in the Circle."

"But some felines consider them great teachers," explained Tiptoe, reminding her brother why they were special.

Beetle thought for a moment. "Mother, does Fat Face have a special place in the Circle?"

"No. As I explained, all are equal in the Circle."

"Is he a great teacher?"

"No!"

"But he has followers."

"Yes, because they are afraid. He steals their power from them and then offers them protection within the Brotherhood."

Tiptoe looked at Beetle and her eyes filled with light. "Fat Face cannot be a great teacher."

Geraldine listened with keen interest. "Why, little one?"

"Fat Face is just clever. A great teacher must be wise."

Chapter 8

One morning Geraldine returned to the den with a mouse dangling from her mouth. She signaled the kittens to follow her to the patio. They formed a circle, and she released the mouse. Initially the creature was dazed. It recovered quickly, darting around the circle with surprising speed, stopping suddenly and changing directions unpredictably in its determined effort to escape. The kittens crouched, swishing their tails nervously, uncertain what to do next.

Geraldine prepared to attack. She remained motionless for some time. She crouched, lashing her tail from side to side, her hindquarters quivering in anticipation. In one fluid motion she charged the mouse and pounced on it, pinning it with her paw. Her unexpected attack startled her kittens. They huddled together, watching spellbound as their mother released the mouse and recaptured it several times. After her demonstration, Geraldine signaled the kittens to re-form their circle. Once again she freed the mouse.

Beetle crept forward tentatively. The mouse froze. Beetle stopped to observe the creature with intense fascination. When he detected no further movement, he glanced around the patio searching for new excitement. The mouse sensed that Beetle's attention had shifted. It broke its statue-like pose and dashed toward the safety of the ivy, only to find Whisper trotting beside it in a friendly, curious manner. It changed direction abruptly and darted boldly across Whisper's path, jumping at him, making a loud, high-pitched sound. Whisper hopped backward in alarm and the mouse bolted into the ivy. Geraldine had positioned herself to promptly retrieve it.

Since Tiptoe had made no move toward the mouse, Geraldine released it near her. Tiptoe hesitated a moment, then lunged at the creature, managing to trap it with her paws. She was astonished by her success. She was just as surprised when she relaxed her grip and the mouse shot forward and escaped.

Once again Geraldine caught the mouse and returned it to her kittens so they could continue practicing. She tensely scrutinized every move, measuring the extent of their progress. She watched her kittens grow in skill and confidence with each successful attack and capture until she was satisfied they had progressed sufficiently.

One final demonstration was necessary. The mouse was now tired enough for Geraldine to move it into position for the killing bite. Once again she prepared to attack. She leapt at the mouse, pinning it down with her forepaws. She moved her nose along the mouse's body and plunged her canine teeth into the back of its neck, severing the spinal chord. The mouse died instantly. Geraldine stepped back from the lifeless body.

Beetle was caught up in the excitement of the chase and continued to bat at the mouse. He scowled furiously at the creature when he got no response. Whisper tapped the mouse lightly with his paw. He jabbed it a little bit harder. Tiptoe also pawed at the still body, trying to elicit some reaction. The kittens looked at their mother inquisitively.

"The creature's body will sleep forever," she explained.

"Why?" asked Whisper.

"I have made it so."

The kittens studied the puncture marks on the mouse's neck and understood. Geraldine settled in next to her prey and began to eat. Beetle and Tiptoe joined her. Whisper did not.

"But, why?" he insisted.

"We must eat to live, and sometimes we must kill to eat."

"But we have plenty to eat."

"For now. You must learn to hunt and to kill on your own just in case we do not."

Whisper was still reluctant. Geraldine looked at him sympathetically, "You must be able to hunt to survive."

"I know."

"It is a feline's responsibility to kill as quickly and as painlessly as possible."

"I know."

"We only chase our prey to tire it so that we can position it for the killing bite. That bite must be precise."

"I understand."

"The hunt requires great skill. Skill requires practice."

Whisper looked away.

"My love, no creature can be caught before its time."

He looked back at his mother soberly. "I will learn to hunt . . . I don't think I will ever like it."

"It is something that must be done, my love. It is not something to enjoy. There are Companions who have forgotten why we kill. They hunt to amuse themselves, not to survive."

Beetle was confident. "It all seems pretty simple to me. You think too much, my brother."

Whisper answered, "And you, brother, think too little!"

Geraldine acted as mediator. "Experience will teach you that knowing and thinking each have their place." She focused her gaze on Beetle. "I assure you, the hunt is not simple. It requires persistence, concentration, and *patience*."

Beetle did not miss the emphasis on patience. He pretended to be unconcerned and casually groomed his glossy coat. Geraldine returned to her meal. Beetle and Tiptoe followed her example. Tiptoe paused for a moment, lost in deep reflection. "Maybe if I don't eat little creatures, big creatures won't eat me."

"My love, if big creatures are hungry and they perceive you as prey, they will try and eat you."

"Oh."

Whisper watched a while longer and then joined his mother and his littermates. Geraldine glanced approvingly at him, convinced that today's lesson was complete. However, Whisper had decided he preferred to find his food in a dish on the patio.

Chapter 9

The days passed without incident. Geraldine and her kittens lived undisturbed on the hilltop. The dishes were always refilled and each day she felt more secure in her new home. She allowed the kittens to eat with her on the patio every morning, and they continued to perfect their hunting skills. As they developed, she began to leave them for longer periods of time. They were still immature, but they were no longer defenseless. Nevertheless, she always elicited a solemn promise from each kitten to remain on the hilltop until she returned.

Geraldine had avoided the rest of the feline community since the birth of her kittens. She was anxious to visit her old haunts and to see her friend Tosey. Geraldine never forgot a kindness, and Tosey's help had enabled her to survive on the streets. Her good friend would also be aware of the latest gossip and eager to tell it.

One morning Geraldine announced that she planned to visit Tosey and that she would be gone from the hilltop most of the afternoon. The kittens found it difficult to understand why they could not go with her.

"Right now, my loves, you must remain here. It is safer for you and for me. When you are older and fully trained I will take you with me. I promise."

"How soon will that be?" Tiptoe asked as usual.

"You must trust me to . . ."

"'Make that decision.' I know. I trust you Mother, but it seems like it's taking us forever to become old enough to make our own decisions. I want to meet a Tree Climber."

"I want to see Father," Whisper added.

Beetle was strangely silent.

"Patience, my loves. Growing up takes time. I only restrict you to keep you safe. Now I need something from each of you."

The kittens understood.

"I will stay on the hilltop until you return," Tiptoe promised.

"So will I," Whisper promised.

Geraldine waited patiently for Beetle's response. He usually stalled until he was certain he could not avoid it.

"All right! All right! I promise."

As Geraldine began her journey, she automatically looked for the brown squirrel. Their paths crossed almost every day. He seemed to accept her presence on the hill and to realize she meant him no harm. He called himself Lightfoot, and he lived in the large tree where she had first seen him. This time he was expertly skimming along the wires that were a regular part of the city landscape. Geraldine was surefooted, but Lightfoot's balance and agility amazed her. She sent him a friendly greeting and he responded enthusiastically. She enjoyed their brief encounters and looked forward to them.

The afternoon was warm and sunny. Geraldine was in awe of the
beauty surrounding her: the large trees, the expanses of lush green
lawn, the lovely flowers neatly arranged by color, releasing their
pleasing fragrance. She felt free for the first time in months—free
from hunger, free from thirst, free from constant threat. She and her
kittens had escaped the dark sterility of the alley into this place filled
with life and light.

Geraldine still had not regained her physical strength, but
her love for her kittens and a deep sense of gratitude for this new
beginning filled her with the energy of sheer joy. She hurried along
the city streets eager to see Tosey. She knew it would be easy to
find her friend. She guessed Tosey would be sunning herself in her
favorite spot at this time of day. However, she caught a familiar
scent on a nearby hedge and changed course abruptly. Fat Face had
passed that way minutes before. He was the last feline she wanted to
encounter, so she prepared to cross the street.

Geraldine's first attempt to cross a busy street had been a
terrifying experience. The objects moving across her path were
huge, fast, and noisy. Instinctively she knew there was no margin
for error. Now the experience had become routine. One car passed,
then another, in quick succession. Geraldine waited patiently for
exactly the right moment, dashed across the street, and disappeared
between two houses. She passed through several backyards and
finally reached a vacant lot.

The area looked much the same as it had months before when
Geraldine and Tosey spent hours together pleasantly hidden in the
weeds and grass. She saw Tosey and two other friends, Butterfly

and Harmony, trotting toward her with their tails held high. They were genuinely happy to see Geraldine and obviously aware of her approach before they saw her. They all touched noses affectionately.

"Where have you been?" Tosey asked, as concerned as she was curious. "We have missed you in the Circle!"

"Oh yes," agreed Butterfly and Harmony almost simultaneously.

Geraldine and her friends sniffed each other thoroughly. "You have little ones," Tosey observed with interest. "I should have known!"

"Oh my." Butterfly was uncertain whether to be happy or sad for Geraldine. Harmony was just as confused by the news. They had both been spayed when they were young so their life experience had been quite different.

"My friends, they are so beautiful!" The light in Geraldine's large green eyes glistened with the love she felt for her kittens. "They need me now to protect them and to teach them."

"I understand," Tosey replied with a hint of sadness. "I once had little ones of my own. But look at you! You are so thin."

Tosey's remark surprised her. Geraldine had always taken pride in her beauty and the admiration it inspired in other felines. She had not thought much about her appearance since the birth of her kittens.

"Life has been hard for us. It's better now." Geraldine told her friends about her good fortune.

"Fat Face asked about you," Tosey added with a gleam in her eye.

"Oh." Geraldine replied flatly, without interest.

Butterfly and Harmony shuddered at the thought of his distorted cheeks, broken whiskers, tattered coat, and odd scent. They clearly shared Geraldine's distaste for him.

Tosey gave Geraldine a friendly, but impatient look. "You still haven't given up on the Great Mother's gift to all females. You'd think he is the only tomcat around."

"He is, Tosey, for me. Do you ever see him?"

"The tall, elegant one?" asked Butterfly.

"With the exquisite set of white brows and whiskers," sighed Harmony, full of admiration for Romeo. "Such dignity. So very feline."

"I see him once in awhile," answered Tosey, "in the Circle, but I hear things all the time."

Geraldine was certain she didn't want to hear those "things."

"Believe me," continued Tosey, "you'll find out one male is as good as another."

"I wish it were that simple for me."

"Forget him."

"I try, Tosey."

"Forget all of them. Males are mostly trouble. There was a time when I lived for a little Pleasure Scent and a lively tom. My life is different now. But it's a good life—in many ways, it's better."

Geraldine was aware that felines sometimes lost their ability to reproduce their own kind when they joined human families. "Maybe it is better, Tosey. I love my little ones. I would give my life for them. So far we have managed to survive, but what about the future? What will become of them? What will become of me?"

"There's only one solution," advised Tosey. "Get the human to take you in."

"But what about my little ones?"

Butterfly and Harmony exchanged a grave look. They were both Companions to the same human. They questioned if any human would accept an entire feline family.

Tosey's habit was to ignore what she did not want to hear, so she continued on. "Good food, shelter, and some Pleasure Scent now and then. Yes, it's a good life."

"I agree. It is a good life. But Tosey, you know the Pleasure Scent is just a trap."

Once again, Tosey ignored her. Geraldine had learned it was useless to press Tosey for a response she did not want to give, so she simply listened. "There are felines like Fat Face who refuse to accept change. Life around us has changed, and we must change—or perish. Yes, my friend, there is only one way: Get the human to take you in." Tosey changed the subject. "So will we see you in the Circle tonight?"

Geraldine hesitated, unwilling to commit herself.

"Well, if not tonight, I hope soon. A Tree Climber visits the Circle now."

"Really!" exclaimed Geraldine.

"The Tree Climbers are renowned for their wisdom," remarked Butterfly.

"She is quite fascinating and most powerful," added Harmony.

"Both wise and powerful?" Geraldine was impressed.

"Oh yes, in ways felines have forgotten."

Tosey was skeptical. "Well, maybe. The Tree Climber shares thoughts that are difficult to accept. We all know the Great Feline exists in the High Place."

"Of course," answered Geraldine.

"Then why does she urge us to search the deepest parts of ourselves?"

Geraldine was interested. "What else?"

"She advises us to be as shrewd as the large rodent, yet as innocent as a newborn. Now how can that be?"

"I have no idea." Geraldine was more curious than ever.

"Anyway, my friend, you must come and decide for yourself." Tosey addressed Butterfly and Harmony. "Will the two of you attend tonight?"

Butterfly and Harmony provided each other with the company of their own kind, so they did not visit the Circle as regularly as some of the other felines.

"Our human has presented us with a special opening to the outside," Butterfly announced proudly.

"We can now come and go as we please." Harmony was enthusiastic about their new freedom.

"What?" Tosey had never heard of such an arrangement.

"Oh, yes, you must come see it. It is most convenient, but it has its advantages and disadvantages," she warned.

Tosey could not imagine any disadvantages. "Wait until the others hear about this!" Tosey was already considering how she could get her human to do the same.

"We may see you tonight, but later. Our human is quite distressed and needs our presence," explained Butterfly. "Once she sleeps . . . maybe then."

The four cats shared their thoughts and feelings for a while longer. Finally, Geraldine knew she must return to her kittens. She wished her friends well. "May the Great Mother be with you."

"And with you," they each responded. They touched noses before leaving and promised to visit with one another again soon.

Geraldine considered Tosey's invitation to attend the gathering that night. Although she looked forward to spending more time with friends and to meeting the Tree Climber, she must wait until her kittens were older and better prepared to survive. Travel after dark was risky, and there could be danger in the Circle. It would be evident to every feline present, including the Brotherhood, that she had become a mother. The Brotherhood would certainly kill her kittens if they had the opportunity.

Chapter 10

The gentle afternoon breeze provided an unexpected delight as Geraldine trotted briskly along the street toward home. She inhaled a potpourri of delicate, spring scents and the appetizing aroma of a barbecue. She glanced at the orange sky, but decided the prize was worth a short delay. If the conditions were just right, she might have the opportunity to repeat a memorable experience.

Geraldine followed the trail of the enticing scent down a familiar driveway. She leapt to the top of a gate, balancing there for a moment to scan the yard below. She spotted her objective immediately and jumped silently into the bushes. She was delighted to see her prize low to the ground and unattended. Two steaks sizzled on an open hibachi, but they had not yet been turned. She had learned from experience that she must act quickly or the meat would become too hot to snatch easily.

Geraldine slinked toward her quarry, alert for any sign of interference. She reached the hibachi, rose up on her haunches, extended her claws, and snagged the steak nearest her. She snagged it again, moving it close to the edge of the grill. She rose up one last time, and with a flick of her claws, pulled it to the ground. It was too hot for her to pick up in her mouth, so she jerked the meat toward the safety of the bushes with several quick, light flicks of her claws. She rested there, well hidden in the dense shrubbery, waiting for her prize to cool.

Geraldine congratulated herself on improving her skill since her first attempts. Gnawing hunger had inspired her original daring. Although she had managed to steal the steak, she singed her fur and burned the tender pads on her paws in the process. However, the prize was worth it. The meat was not only tasty, but she delighted the other cats in the Circle with the telling and retelling of her adventure. Geraldine now enjoyed a certain status among them because no other feline had duplicated her feat.

A man suddenly appeared on the patio. Geraldine automatically hugged the ground and remained motionless. He called to someone in the house, and a woman joined him. She watched them gesture anxiously to each other, glancing around the yard, trying to determine the fate of the missing steak. Geraldine was amazed. The humans were unaware of her presence. She was well hidden, but close enough for any other creature to detect her scent in an instant. "Humans are such strange creatures," she thought, "so big, so strong, and yet, so vulnerable."

The humans did not intend to leave the second steak unprotected. Geraldine waited patiently. When they finally disappeared into the house, she ate heartily, savoring every morsel. It would be a long time before she could strike again. She had learned to respect human intelligence. If she raided them too often they would find a way to protect against her thievery.

Geraldine arrived home just before sunset. As she trotted in the direction of her den she heard the excited chatter of squirrels. She wondered if Lightfoot and some of his friends were playing in the partial clearing under the tree where he lived. Geraldine jumped onto an ivy-covered stump so she could satisfy her curiosity. She saw her spirited friend romping and tumbling gleefully with another squirrel identical in coloring, but smaller in size. "Lightfoot has a mate," observed Geraldine.

Lightfoot and his mate chased each other around the tree several times and ran toward a large bush. They stopped abruptly, Lightfoot lunged forward, and both squirrels ran as fast as their legs could carry them in the opposite direction. Geraldine stared in blank astonishment as a small black figure sprang from the bush in hot pursuit. "Beetle!" She called furiously. Beetle vanished immediately in the direction of the den.

Geraldine's outcry frightened Lightfoot's mate. She scampered part way up the tree trunk and froze. He remained at the bottom of the tree, murmuring to her reassuringly. Geraldine jumped to the ground and approached him slowly. "I am sorry," she apologized. My little one has so much energy that sometimes he uses it at the wrong time and the wrong place."

Lightfoot seemed puzzled. Then he gave her an amused, impish look. "My friend, we sensed your little one watching us from a distance. We thought it would be great fun to encourage him to chase us. We enjoyed the play as much as he did."

Geraldine began to understand. She recognized her own arrogance.

"Don't be angry with him. His energy is amazing!" Lightfoot added, "I assure you he will sleep peacefully tonight."

Geraldine's eyes danced with laughter.

The kittens greeted their mother with a chorus of mews when she entered the den. They sniffed her with real interest because she had been somewhere different. Geraldine stood for a moment, purring softly, gently kneading the leaves beneath her feet, happy to be with her family again in the security of her den. She circled herself several times, searching for exactly the right spot, and stretched out on the soft leaves. Beetle gave her a sheepish look as he snuggled close to her.

"Our friend Lightfoot told me you had great fun together this afternoon."

"Oh, yes!" Beetle was obviously relieved. "You should have seen me, Mother. I'm quick and strong and soon I'll be big enough to climb trees and . . ."

Geraldine was about to repeat her mother's warning about climbing trees, but decided against it. Beetle never finished his thought. He nestled his head a little deeper into his mother's soft, thick fur and was fast asleep. Whisper rubbed his head against her neck, and she licked him affectionately. Geraldine noticed that Tiptoe seemed reluctant to join them. She approached her mother slowly. As she came closer, Geraldine jumped to her feet in alarm.

"The human has touched you!"

"Yes, Mother."

"I warned you not to trust humans until they prove themselves."

"We were playing, and she was suddenly just there."

Geraldine was stunned. The woman had never attempted to climb the hill. She only spent enough time on the patio to refill the dishes. She knew Geraldine came down to the patio to eat, but never disturbed her. Geraldine fought against the panic spreading through her body. She quieted herself, allowed the Knowing to guide her, and returned her attention to the story Tiptoe was telling.

"Beetle and Whisper ran back to the den. I started to follow. When Whisper was no longer watching me, I stopped. Mother, I decided not to run away."

"You what?"

"Oh, at first I was frightened. The human is a giant creature. It was impossible for me to see all of her at one time. But Mother, the light around her body was clear and bright. She approached me slowly and let me sniff her. She gently reached toward me to stroke my fur."

Once again, Geraldine quelled the panic she felt. It would only distort her intuition.

Tiptoe continued, "The next thing I knew she lifted me up, just like you do."

Geraldine was so threatened by the fact that the human had touched her kitten she could barely contain her fear.

"She spoke to me softly and placed me close to her body. It was so pleasant, Mother. Then I became afraid. I knew you would be angry with me. I started to squirm. Mother, she put me down immediately, and I ran as fast as I could. I did not go back to the den right away. I hid. I didn't want her to find Beetle and Whisper, too."

"And then what happened?" Geraldine was still upset, but proud of Tiptoe's foresight and courage.

"The human did not try to follow me. I waited until I heard the final sound, proceeded cautiously, just as you taught us, and joined Whisper and Beetle. I liked being with her, Mother. I know she would never harm us."

The kittens waited tensely for their mother to decide what she would do next.

Geraldine was not only threatened by the human scent she detected on her kitten, she was alarmed because the woman must have climbed the hill. Nevertheless, her deepest instinct was to remain on the hilltop, and she trusted her guidance. She still felt compelled to warn Tiptoe, "If the human tries to approach you again when I am not here, you run back to the den immediately! Promise me, little one."

Tiptoe looked away and did not respond. Geraldine was shocked. Tiptoe had such an intense desire to please; she never defied her mother.

"Tiptoe, promise me!"

Tiptoe still did not respond.

"Promise me . . . just until I am certain there is no danger."

Tiptoe looked up at her mother with her deep, mystical eyes. "All right. I promise. But, Mother, I feel humans need us for more than our hunting skills."

As Geraldine and her kittens arranged and rearranged themselves into comfortable sleeping positions, a clear picture flashed through her mind, prompting her to ask Tiptoe one last question.

"Tiptoe."

"Yes, Mother."

"Did you leave the hilltop during my absence?"

"Yes, Mother."

"Were you at the bottom of the hill when you saw the human?"

"Yes."

"Tiptoe, you promised me!"

"I know. I am sorry."

"And you Whisper?"

"Yes, Mother."

"Beetle?"

"Yes." He gave his littermates an accusing look. "I told you she would know!"

Geraldine was hurt and confused by her kittens' disobedience. All three of them had broken their promise to her. More important, she could not protect them if they did not obey her. She sat quietly observing each of them, waiting for guidance. Their tiny bodies and faces had looked so much alike when they were first born. She marveled at how quickly they had changed over the past few months. Each had become an individual.

When the answer came, it was simple. She had been able to protect them until now. She could not protect them forever. They must gradually transfer the trust they had placed in her to trust in themselves. They were ready for this change.

Chapter 11

The next morning Geraldine and her kittens made their routine trip to the patio for their meal. She saw Lightfoot sitting on the fence proudly grooming his impressive tail.

"Hello! Did the little one sleep well last night?"

"Yes," responded Geraldine.

"Mother, I am going to stay here and play."

"We are going to eat now."

"I'm not hungry."

"You will be."

"I don't care. I want to play."

Geraldine considered picking Beetle up by the scruff of his neck, but she controlled the impulse. She looked for Lightfoot and was relieved to see that he had disappeared.

"Our friend apparently has something else to do. Besides, Whisper and Tiptoe want to play with you."

"But, Mother, they are so slow!"

"Maybe so, but they are already at the bottom of the hill waiting to eat."

Beetle suddenly felt he had been left behind and dashed down the hill to join his littermates.

When Geraldine reached the patio, Tiptoe called to her mother excitedly. Geraldine saw three bowls of food next to the water dish. One of the extra bowls was filled with milk.

Tiptoe's large eyes glowed with the joy she felt at this discovery. "Now do you believe me?"

Geraldine was still troubled by Tiptoe's desire to trust the human. She was not prepared to give her full approval. She ate a few bites, then retreated to a spot under the tree to groom herself and let the kittens have their fill.   They only squabbled once over the milk. She was grateful their manners finally showed some sign of improvement.

After the kittens finished eating and grooming, Tiptoe remained next to her mother. Beetle studied a group of ants crawling back and forth across the patio, preparing to attack and scatter their orderly columns. Whisper sat quietly near the wild roses observing a spider web glistening in the sunlight. His white and black coat was striking against the green foliage and the bright red blossoms.

Whisper's coloring concerned Geraldine as much as it pleased her. It would make him more vulnerable to predators and highly visible to prey. An exotic coat was an asset for a Companion like Romeo. His beauty seemed to make him more precious to his humans. However, Whisper might have to survive on the streets.

Later that evening the sound of human voices floated toward the den and woke Geraldine and her kittens. The sounds were distant at first, but quickly grew louder. She licked each kitten reassuringly until they fell back to sleep.

This was not the first time the woman had visitors on the lower patio. Geraldine had weighed the risk and resisted her curiosity about the voices. However, she realized her innate distrust of humans was interfering with her natural ability to Know. She seized this opportunity to study the woman for a considerable length of time.

Geraldine slipped away from her kittens and made her way cautiously to the bottom of the hill. She snuck across the patio, protected by the twilight, and peered through the shrubbery. Her ears moved back and forth alertly.

The woman was seated with several visitors at the table on the lower patio. Geraldine relaxed, focusing her attention on the light around the woman's body. She was also attentive to her gestures and the tone of her voice. She scrutinized the woman's interaction with each of the other humans. At first, the conversation meant nothing to her and merely tried her patience. In time, vivid pictures appeared in her mind and she was able to sense some of the woman's thoughts and feel her more intense emotions.

Geraldine was encouraged by her observations. The woman's sounds, gestures, thoughts, and feelings were generally in harmony. She spoke from her heart most of the evening. There was one instance in which Geraldine was certain the woman was hiding her true feelings. One of the humans at the table touched her hand. The light around her body expanded and glowed intensely, yet she gave no other indication that the person was of importance to her.

Geraldine focused her concentration on the multitude of stars scattered overhead, hoping for just one reassuring glimpse of the Great Feline. "Will this human continue to offer us friendship rather than betrayal?" she asked, opening her heart to guidance. "Is it possible Tiptoe has been right all along? Should I take Tosey's advice?"

Geraldine reconsidered an idea she had kept at the edge of her mind. The human might accept at least one of her kittens as a Companion. Beetle still insisted on becoming a Street Dweller. However, both Whisper and Tiptoe seemed to prefer the life of a Companion. "When the time comes," she concluded, "we must make this decision together."

Geraldine entered the den and stretched out beside her kittens. Beetle opened his eyes and yawned. He thrust his ears forward and listened for a moment. "The humans are finally gone!" He stood, stretched slowly, and lay down again. "How did you ever learn to understand any of those silly sounds they make?"

"It wasn't easy," admitted Geraldine. "It took time and patience . . . and love."

Tiptoe sat up. She rubbed her head against her mother's shoulder. "Love makes everything easier, doesn't it, Mother?"

"Oh, yes, little one."

Tiptoe disturbed Whisper, and he rolled lazily onto his side. He arched his body backward in a long, luxurious stretch. "But they use so many sounds," he complained.

"Humans rely on sounds and gestures to communicate, little one."

Whisper snuggled closer to his mother. "Do humans ever share thoughts and feelings without using sounds . . . like felines and other creatures do?"

"The Tree Climbers tell the story of a human who lived in another place, long before my mother's time, or her mother's time, who possessed this ability. He considered all of us his sisters and his brothers."

Tiptoe listened with interest. "That human understood all creatures and they understood him?"

"Yes, according to the Tree Climbers."

Beetle sat up very straight. "There is nothing that a human could think or feel that would interest me."

"My love, you must never close your mind. All creatures can learn from one another. We must always watch and listen."

"Humans are too complicated to understand," Beetle insisted.

"Does a Companion have to learn all of their sounds?" asked Whisper, exhausted by the thought of it.

"No. You will automatically learn some of them. Just treat humans as you would any other creature. Observe the light around the body . . ."

"'Feel the vibrations flowing from it,'" Beetle added, with as little enthusiasm as possible.

Whisper was proud of his knowledge. "'Watch every gesture.'"

There was a pause.

"What else, little ones?"

"'Listen to the tone of their sounds,'" Tiptoe answered, enjoying the game.

"Yes, my loves." Geraldine was impressed. "You can normally sense what the human is thinking and feeling with these clues."

Tiptoe tilted her dainty head to one side and gave her mother a questioning look. "How do we let the human know what we are thinking and feeling?"

"That is more difficult. I was able to share thoughts with the little human in my family because his heart was open to me. This was rarely possible with the mother human and father human. I had to use sounds and gestures to get my message across to them. And I had to be clever and persistent. It took a great deal of intelligence and skill to make them understand I was trying to tell them something."

"It seems to me," Beetle concluded, "that humans don't know much of anything. They're not smart. They're just big."

"Well," Geraldine nuzzled him good-naturedly, "you understand now that size is not the measure of a creature. However, never underestimate humans, my love. They are clever."

Chapter 12

One afternoon while her kittens were napping, Geraldine felt restless and decided to go for a walk. She looked for her friend Lightfoot as she climbed down the hill. She did not see him as often now that he had a mate. She missed his friendly presence.

It was a splendid afternoon. Gray clouds had concealed the sun earlier. Now it shone with a dazzling brilliance. Geraldine responded to the feel of its warmth on her coat, allowing it to penetrate her entire being. She experienced an immediate surge of new energy.

Geraldine had not seen Gorgeous for a while so she decided to pay her a visit. She found her reclining in the window as usual. She looked as if she had not moved since the last time Geraldine saw her.

"How are you?" Geraldine asked.

"I am carrying new life!" she answered proudly.

"Wonderful!"

"The little ones will arrive soon. Where have you been? I have missed your visits."

Geraldine had never mentioned her kittens to Gorgeous. "I have little ones of my own."

"Oh, my! Out there! All alone!"

"It has not been easy for us."

"I don't even want to imagine."

"We have help now."

"Have you found humans to take you in?"

"No, but a human puts food out for us each day."

"That's a beginning. Be smart. Get inside where it is safe, and stay there!"

"Well . . . maybe." Geraldine was still not certain she would want to live like Gorgeous. She saw little left in her new friend that she could identify as feline.

Gorgeous rearranged her huge bulk into a more comfortable position. "I will not be here to visit with you for a while. My humans are most attentive, but as you know, little ones take time."

"Yes they do," agreed Geraldine. "Soon mine will begin new lives without me. I will miss them very much. However, I will be able to visit with you more often."

"I look forward to seeing you. Keep yourself safe."

Geraldine trotted happily along the streets, appreciating the beauty around her, grateful for another day of life. She caught the scent first, and then looked to her left involuntarily. She did not want to believe her eyes! A small creature was lying near the center of the street. She was certain it was Lightfoot. For a moment she thought she detected movement. A soft breeze had merely ruffled Lightfoot's fluffy, plume-like tail. Geraldine ran to her friend and gently nuzzled him. She got no response, so she pushed hard against his body, confirming what she already knew. His body would sleep forever. She felt the heavy vibrations of an approaching automobile so she scampered back to the curb. She mourned her friend there, and then slowly walked away.

Geraldine deliberately lost herself in the songs of the creatures around her and the brightly colored landscape. She lifted her elegant head, opening her mouth slightly to deeply savor the fragrances the gentle wind carried her way. She felt better instantly. She continued to walk, with no particular destination, and found herself once again in her old haunts.

"Hello!" a high, shrill voice called to her.

Geraldine was in territory claimed by a Companion named Honey Bee. Geraldine considered her the most unpleasant feline she had ever met. She was part Siamese, and she was arrogant about both her ancestry and her lifestyle. Tosey called her the Stinker, a most insulting nickname. Felines abhor strong, offensive odor. However, Honey Bee was a formidable opponent, so the nickname was a well-kept secret, used only behind her back. Geraldine was in no mood to deal with the Stinker. However, it was not easy to escape her once she saw you.

"It has been a long time!" Honey Bee thoroughly scrutinized Geraldine. "You look awful!"

Honey Bee droned on. She was as full of the latest gossip as Tosey, but she lacked Tosey's innate kindness. She used sounds as liberally as she did thoughts, and at such a pace that Geraldine quickly tired of the conversation. She paid as little attention as possible and was happy to bid Honey Bee a polite farewell.

As Geraldine walked through a part of her old territory, wrapped in fond memories, she surrendered to an irresistible impulse. A few minutes later she jumped down from a fence into a beautiful garden full of sunshine and growing things. The lawn was smooth and green. The flowers were alive with color and fragrance. Geraldine loved this place. It was Romeo's favorite backyard, and it was where they had sealed their friendship. She stretched out luxuriously on the cool grass, indulging her desire to remember. A gentle breeze blew against her face, and she allowed its touch to free her spirit. She floated backward in time, returning to the carefree, play-filled days she spent with her mother and her littermates. She relived treasured memories of the little human, his gentle touch, the feel of his love. And—she remembered Romeo.

Geraldine had met Romeo shortly after she was abandoned. She was frightened, lonely, and of course, hungry. She crept through a field of grass in a vacant lot, confused by these unfamiliar feelings, uncertain how to ease the gnawing hunger, when she sensed the presence of another cat. She turned and saw Romeo for the first time.

Romeo was the most beautiful feline Geraldine had ever seen. He was tall and slender. His chalk white coat was immaculately groomed. His tail was black, long, and full. Black spilled over his head and ears, separated midpoint on his forehead, and cascaded down the sides of his head into a prominent, white ruff, dramatizing his elegantly contoured face, lush white whiskers, and striking gold eyes rimmed in black. He greeted her in a poised, dignified manner with a voice that was rich and deep. Her heart began to beat a little faster, and she licked at her coat nervously.

"You are a newcomer," he began, purring softly.

Geraldine struggled to maintain her dignity, but she sensed that Romeo was already aware of her reaction to him. She finally managed to overcome her shy, awkward feelings.

"I just arrived."

"How should I address you?"

Geraldine hesitated. There was no feline equivalent for the name humans had given her.

Romeo understood instantly. He had also been given such a name. He observed her thoroughly, from the top of her ears to the tips of her paws, with obvious admiration. Geraldine had always been proud that other felines appreciated her beauty. However, she was embarrassed by his attention. It did not matter. Romeo was so gentle and mannerly that she soon felt she had known him forever.

The following afternoon Geraldine rushed to the exact spot where they had met, at precisely the same time, and found Romeo waiting for her. Every day they lazed together in hidden places, enchanted with each other's presence. However, when the moment arrived, Romeo left her promptly to resume his life as a Companion. On the day Geraldine would always remember, he chose to stay with her the entire afternoon, and at twilight, he brought her here.

The garden was filled with exciting discovery and the promise of sweet memory. Romeo led Geraldine through a paradise of scent and color to a large pond where koi and goldfish lived. She had never witnessed such a sight. Her excitement mounted as she watched the fish scatter here and there through their water world. She instinctively dipped her paw into the clear pool, but withdrew it quickly, satisfied to merely observe the spectacle of color and movement. Romeo leaned down cautiously to drink and encouraged her to join him. He assured her that the taste was a rare treat. She was thirsty enough to overcome her skepticism and was pleasantly surprised.

As they finally stretched out on the smooth lawn and shared

their most secret thoughts, she felt Romeo study her deeply. They
withdrew into an easy silence, and then he asked, "Shall we call each
other, Friend?"

Friendship was a highly respected commitment outside the
Brotherhood. There was no greater honor between a male and a
female.

"Oh, yes!" The response slipped from Geraldine so easily and
with such enthusiasm that she was embarrassed and fell silent. She
followed feline custom and lowered her head, permitting him to
tenderly groom her crown and forehead. She rested her brow against
his silky ruff, and they sat together, with eyes half closed, purring
their contentment.

The sky slowly darkened to provide the enchantment of
starlight, and a moonrise illuminated the entire garden in a
phosphorescent glow. Romeo and Geraldine strolled along a path
that meandered through the garden to a special place where every
growing thing was remarkable for its fragrance. They reclined
together beneath a window box overflowing with jasmine, merging
its delicate perfume with the heavily scented night air. The heady
mix of sweet scents was intoxicating to their sensual, feline natures.

Geraldine was overwhelmed, and she began to sing. Romeo
answered her with his own voluptuous song. The window above
them slammed shut, but this only disrupted their magic for a
moment. They dashed across the garden into a gazebo and lay side by
side among diamonds of moonlight filtering through the lattice roof.

Other tomcats had approached Geraldine. She rejected their
impatient, aggressive behavior. Romeo's sensitivity matched her

own. He made no move toward her for some time. Then he gently placed his paw on hers, and Geraldine's heart belonged to him forever.

The movement of the sun drew Geraldine back to the present, reminding her of her responsibilities. She enjoyed a long, luscious stretch and glanced around the garden one last time. She tucked her memories away neatly and resolved to immerse herself again in her normal routine.

Chapter 13

Geraldine's kittens were oblivious to the shadows the late afternoon sun cast upon the hillside. They seized every opportunity to escape their mother's watchful eye, delighting in the freedom to romp and explore on their own. They finally lay panting in the ivy, exhausted by their play, and realized the sun had disappeared from the sky. Their mother had always returned before sunset. Beetle, Whisper, and Tiptoe shared the same apprehensive feeling. They made their way back to the den and huddled together, waiting impatiently.

Tiptoe pricked her ears, swinging her elegant head in the direction of the patio. Beetle and Whisper lifted their heads attentively. All three kittens kept their bodies still. The sounds from the patio were familiar, but they remained motionless. They listened with all of their senses just as their mother had taught them. Beetle and Whisper relaxed slightly, left the den, and inched their way to the edge of the hill. Tiptoe followed close behind. They were prepared to retreat to the den at the slightest provocation. They pressed close together in the protective covering of the ivy, watching tensely as the woman filled the dishes on the patio, gathered up her bags and cans, and disappeared down the stairs. The kittens sat quietly while they decided what to do next. Although their mother had allowed them more and more freedom, she had forbidden them to play or eat on the patio without her.

Beetle bounded down the hill, hesitating only to decide which dish to tackle first. Whisper was torn between his desire to eat and his desire to obey his mother. The sound of his brother lapping milk resolved his conflict. He paused to take in the scents and sounds around him, and sensed for the first time without his mother's assurance, that he was safe. He decided to trust this new feeling and crept down the hill.

Tiptoe watched in horror. "Whisper! Beetle! We promised!" Her brothers ignored her objection. They were totally absorbed in their meal. Tiptoe was certain there would be no food left unless she joined them immediately. She inhaled deeply and slinked down to the patio.

Geraldine observed her kittens from a distance with mixed feelings. She was pleased for the most part. They were beginning to trust their own instincts. She knew she must also trust in order to support their independence. Beetle should have been more cautious. Tiptoe could have been less timid. Whisper had used the skills she taught him appropriately. Yet, once again, her kittens had made a promise and broken it.

Movement in the large tree where Lightfoot had made his home attracted Geraldine's attention. She automatically expected to see him playfully moving through the branches. What she saw displaced the lingering sadness in her heart and filled her with profound joy. Lightfoot's mate paused at the entrance to her nest to give Geraldine a friendly glance. Clinging to her body, were two baby squirrels!

Geraldine eagerly returned her greeting and then refocused her attention on the patio. However, her kittens were nowhere in sight.

Tiptoe had sounded the alarm. She knew her mother was nearby. Neither Whisper nor Beetle questioned her intuition. They all raced back to the den and began to casually groom themselves. They greeted their mother as usual and sniffed her with curiosity. She carried several unfamiliar scents.

"Where did you go today? Why are you so late?" they mewed in unison.

"So many questions!" Geraldine was amused at first. Then she remembered this was the first time she had returned after sunset. "Were you frightened because I returned late?" she asked them lovingly.

"No," Beetle responded immediately.

"Well, just a little," Whisper admitted with more honesty.

"I was frightened." Tiptoe cuddled next to her mother, instantly reassured by her presence.

"There is no need to worry. I will always come home to you until the day we celebrate the beginning of your new lives."

"Oh, yes!" Beetle responded with intense excitement.

Whisper and Tiptoe were less enthusiastic. Geraldine saw fear in their eyes. "It will be a joyous time for each of you and an occasion of great pride for me. Your lives will be filled with beginnings and endings, endings and beginnings."

Geraldine laid her cheek against the side of their soft faces and felt their fears slowly dissolve in the warmth of her love. "Now, would you like to go down the hill to finish your meal?"

The kittens looked at one another with eyes full of twinkle and mischief.

"No matter. I am pleased. You are making more decisions for yourself. You must trust them. I must trust them! I want you to be prepared. However . . ."

Tiptoe gave her mother a doleful look. "We broke our promise."

"Take responsibility for your promises, my loves. If you make them, keep them. A broken promise is always disappointing."

The kittens followed Geraldine back to the patio. She ate first as usual, but was not particularly hungry. She reclined on the warm cement under an umbrella of pink blossoms and groomed herself, watching their bellies swell with good food, deeply content with their progress.

Geraldine felt her heart would burst with love at the sight of these three small creatures who had passed through her body into life. She saw something of herself in each of them and something of their father, Romeo. She soon discovered she was unable to separate herself from the memories she had so freely indulged that afternoon. Geraldine resigned herself to the only possible solution.

The Circle

Chapter 14

Romeo marveled at the image in the mirror. "That's me," he thought, " . . . or is it?" He calmly observed a feline identical to himself observing him. He murmured and reached out with his paw to touch his twin, withdrawing it quickly when the image mimicked him. He reached out again, and their paws met, but he felt no life in the touch. He sat back, staring at the image, fascinated by the mystery of the mirror.

The pop of an opening can diverted Romeo's attention; he responded at once. Romeo loved to eat. He loved all of his comforts. He strolled through the maze of fragile objects on the dresser with an incredible lightness and jumped gracefully to the floor, gliding down the stairs to the kitchen just as his human summoned him. He paused to affectionately nuzzle his friend, a large, white German shepherd stretched out on the kitchen floor.

Romeo had bonded with the canine from the moment he joined the household as a kitten. He eased his loneliness for his mother and his littermates by falling asleep with his muzzle buried in the soft hair of the shepherd's belly or tucked securely in the hollow under his forearm. The shepherd allowed him to crawl the length and breadth of his huge body, biting his ears, and attacking his tail. Romeo's teeth and claws were tiny, but sharp. The shepherd gently mouthed him, but never hurt him. Their friendship continued to deepen as Romeo matured. They slept side by side each day and with their humans at night, cradled in the folds of a down coverlet—secure, accepted, and loved.

Romeo approached his dish enthusiastically. He sniffed his food, as usual, before eating. He sniffed a second time and stepped back in disbelief. "Not again!" he thought. His owner had recently tampered with his food. Romeo made it quite clear that the new food was unacceptable. He was indignant that his human would make the same mistake again. "My humans are generally clever, responsive, quick to learn. I don't understand . . . such puzzling creatures." Nevertheless, he resolved to be patient.

Romeo considered several ways to adequately display his discontent and selected one that would deliver his message clearly, without sacrificing a meal. He pawed at the floor around his dish as if he were covering excrement in his cat pan. He stopped and looked up. He could see and feel his human's concern. "Excellent! I have her attention." Next he focused all of the disappointment and betrayal he could possibly feel into his large gold eyes. When he felt his human's concern deepen sufficiently, he turned with great drama and walked away from his dish. He sat very still, waiting for the desired response. A moment later he heard the pop of a second can and sniffed the aroma of his favorite food. He dashed toward his human, rewarding her instantly with a rush of loving sounds and repeated caresses with his soft, silky body.

Romeo finished his meal and rejoined his human, lifting his front paws to push against her leg gently. He meowed urgently and ran toward the laundry room. The routine was familiar to both of them, and his human followed obediently. Romeo looked back several times just to make sure she did not stray. He watched her remove the familiar objects from the shelf and trotted ahead of her to the living room, anticipating the exquisite feel of the comb and the brush. He stretched out luxuriously on the hassock and allowed his human to groom him. As she methodically made her way from his head to his tail, he slipped into a place of total relaxation and made plans for his escape.

Romeo was never allowed outside after dark, but periodically he desired the company of his own kind. Tonight he intended to visit the Circle. He knew he would have a split-second opportunity to escape when the other human returned home. Past experience had taught him to use the element of surprise and move suddenly.

Moments before the second human arrived, Romeo positioned himself to one side of the front door, listening closely to footsteps, the turn of the lock, the creak of the door. He tensed his body, preparing to lunge forward. With a flawless sense of timing, he surged past the human and disappeared into the twilight. He heard human voices pleading with him to return. He felt the pleading turn to anger, but there was no way to make them understand. He knew he would be forgiven by the time he returned home and meowed at the bedroom window to be let inside.

Romeo shut out the sound of human voices and looked for his new friend. He saw her peek around the hedge at the end of the driveway. She was called Raindrop because she enjoyed a pastime most felines chose to avoid. She loved to sit in the rain. Although she was a newcomer, she was already celebrated in the Circle for the clear, luminous quality of her pale blue eyes, her exquisite form, and her pure white satin coat. Romeo, like most felines, possessed a highly developed appreciation of beauty, and he delighted in her presence.

Raindrop had been born beautiful, sensitive, and highly intelligent. She was admired by human and feline alike. She possessed the kind of beauty that has inspired artists through the centuries to draw, to paint, and to sculpt. She was perfection itself to the untutored eye. Her breeder soon discovered a flaw that made her unacceptable as a show cat or as breeding stock, so she was sold as a pet. Her new owners treasured her, and she led a privileged life. They provided her with a special room equipped with carpeted, brightly colored ramps, cat trees, scratching posts, a plush bed, plenty of kitty grass, catnip, and a caretaker.

Both humans treated Raindrop with such kindness, she wondered how they could be so cruel to each other. Their relationship swung from indifference to rage. She hid when they raged and reappeared when they lapsed into indifference. After a frightening argument, one of the humans left and never returned. Raindrop became increasingly nervous and distraught over the sudden, daily changes that followed. Furniture was rearranged or disappeared entirely. Strangers constantly streamed in and out of her home. She ended this chapter of her life as bewildered and deeply depressed as her human by their sudden change of fortune. Her world continued to disintegrate until the day her caretaker took her home to join her new family.

Once again Raindrop's life changed dramatically in ways she could never have imagined. Her new world was far from perfect, but she found it so thrilling and inspiring she considered the trade off worth it. She discovered the beauty of the natural world, an endless variety of fellow creatures, and the pastime that delighted her beyond her wildest dreams. She also discovered Romeo.

Raindrop marveled at Romeo's innate grace and elegance as she watched him approach. They greeted each other hastily and dashed off together, wondering who else might visit the Circle that night.

Chapter 15

Two cats, one a tortoiseshell and the other charcoal-gray, slept peacefully entwined on the arm of a cat tree. Butterfly woke first, anticipating the arrival of their human. She gently groomed the crown of her partner's head, smiling inside at the strange sound of her friend's purr.

"Yes," she thought, "most unusual."

At first, Butterfly was greatly offended that her human expected her to share their life with a second feline. She needed constant reassurance to believe that there was room in her human's heart for both of them. She discovered that their life was enhanced rather than diminished by Harmony's presence.

Butterfly nudged Harmony gently. "Wake up! She's here." Harmony reluctantly opened her eyes and rose to her haunches. She was still fairly new to the household and gratefully followed Butterfly's lead.

Both cats jumped to the floor and rushed downstairs to greet their human, weaving in and out of her legs as she reached down to stroke each of them. They trotted behind the woman into the kitchen and sat at her feet, staring up at her with devotion and anticipation.

"She seems fine to me," observed Harmony, hoping that Butterfly would agree. "Surely we can visit the Circle tonight."

Butterfly sighed. "She is still very upset. In time you will learn to recognize the signs."

"Still?" thought Harmony, deeply disappointed. She understood Butterfly's preoccupation with their human's departures and arrivals. When she departed, they ate. When she arrived, they ate. She did not understand her constant concern about the human's physical and emotional well-being. They watched the woman open the refrigerator, quickly scan the contents, remove something, and place it on the countertop. Butterfly followed their human into the living room, where the woman collapsed into a large chair. Harmony remained in the kitchen.

Butterfly looked back. "Come on. What are you waiting for?" Harmony reluctantly trotted into the living room while Butterfly scrutinized the woman from head to toe. "Yes, my friend, our human is still distressed. She needs our attention. Well?" Butterfly waited. "Go ahead."

"But," protested Harmony, "she hasn't fed us yet."

"Oh my, didn't you observe what she is going to eat?"

"No."

Butterfly sighed again. "In time you will become more observant. What she consumes is far more pleasing to our senses than what she normally gives us to eat. Trust me. Do as I have instructed you. She will share her meal with us, and we will visit the Circle!"

Harmony's life had accustomed her to scarcity. She found it difficult to pass up a certainty for a possibility. Furthermore, her limited experience with humans convinced her that they must be pestered relentlessly to obtain a desired response. Nevertheless, she was learning to trust her friend's understanding of human behavior, at least of this particular human. "Help me to remember what I must do."

Butterfly gave her an amused look. "All right. But remember, it's not just about doing. If you just do and don't feel, you will only experience frustration. The doing must come from your heart to bring you joy."

"More Tree Climber wisdom," thought Harmony wearily.

Butterfly knew it would take time and experience for her friend to understand. She remained patient. "Yes, it is Tree Climber wisdom. It is honorable to serve. Give abundantly, receive abundantly."

Harmony was skeptical. "A feline . . . a servant? Give abundantly and you may have nothing left for yourself!"

"Try this new way," urged Butterfly. "You will be pleasantly surprised."

Harmony resigned herself to the inevitable. "What comes first?"

"Jump onto her legs."

Harmony hesitated. Humans had punished her in the past for such behavior.

"Go ahead. There is nothing to fear. Gently now."

Harmony landed softly on the woman's lap. Instinctively she pushed against the woman's body with her front paws.

"That's it!" Butterfly encouraged her. "Remember, gently."

Harmony found the experience most pleasing and purred loudly. The woman immediately responded to the odd sound of her purr and smiled broadly, stroking her affectionately.

"Perfect," observed Butterfly. "Can you feel the tension leave her body and your own? Purr as loud as you can. Now, nuzzle her. She loves that!"

The woman was visibly pleased, and Harmony was delighted with the result of her effort.

"Yes!" Butterfly's eyes sparkled with enthusiasm. "The three of us will work well together. You will see. Now, find a comfortable position next to her body and I will begin."

Harmony snuggled close to the woman and watched Butterfly perform a similar ritual. "Is it possible we will share the human's meal and visit the Circle tonight?" she wondered. "And will this happen because we did something for our human that gave her pleasure and gave us pleasure, too?" Harmony struggled to accept the possibility of such good fortune.

Chapter 16

F at Face lounged peacefully with a few of his fellow strays among the headstones of an old cemetery. The city had expanded around it, and eventually a larger tract of land was set aside for burials across town. Now there were occasional curiosity seekers, but no visitors. This relic of the past was home to the Brotherhood, a colony of Street Dwellers. There was no longer enough prey to support them, so they scavenged in the alleys behind nearby restaurants and raided the garbage cans of local residents.

Fat Face appeared to be resting. Like his Brothers, he was acutely aware of all that surrounded him. He shielded his thoughts, deeply scrutinizing each of his potential rivals. He enjoyed speculating who might dare to challenge him next. He observed a shorthaired, gray tabby nibble at a few shoots of grass that managed to push their way to the surface after the recent rain.

"That?" Fat Face laughed inside at the thought. "Never! Too small . . . too weak . . . he has no name."

No name had been the runt of his litter and had never grown to full adult size. He was a poor hunter and lacked cunning, so he was not only small, but also thin and malnourished.

Fat Face watched Dog Chaser paw vigorously at the side of

his head. "Perhaps Dog Chaser. He possesses the strength and the courage."

Dog Chaser was a large cat, like Fat Face. His daring was legendary. Brilliant aqua-colored eyes added panache to his otherwise ordinary appearance, making him a favorite with the females.

"Ah, but pleasure is his master. Adventure is his passion," mused Fat Face. "No tenacity!"

Dog Chaser temporarily eliminated the source of his discomfort and lay back with his eyes half closed, purring contentedly.

"And what about you, Rat Eater? You have the strength, the courage, and the intelligence."

Rat Eater was medium-sized, lean, and well muscled. He stopped grooming his pale, marmalade coat, aware that he was being observed. His face had a pointed look like the large rats he was famous for hunting and killing. He fixed his cool gaze on Fat Face.

Fat Face focused all of his power into his narrow green eyes, returning his rival's stare. "You are also cunning. Yes," thought Fat Face with deep amusement, "you will certainly be next."

An inner clock signaled Fat Face to leave for the Circle. He looked forward to these gatherings. They provided him with the opportunity to exercise his power. He found that most satisfying. Without taking his eyes from Rat Eater, he gestured to Dog Chaser that it was time to depart. Rat Eater used this as an excuse to break eye contact without losing face.

"Where are we going?" asked no name.

Before Fat Face could respond, a wretched feline, ravaged by age and life on the streets, began to cough and to heave. The old one had once been as magnificent in his strength as Fat Face. Now his body was a scramble of lumps and sores, the twisted mats on his thick, soiled fur pulling mercilessly at his tender skin. He had been stripped of his name and spent most of his time alone and hungry with nowhere to turn for relief or compassion. He was an embarrassment to the Brotherhood whose code valued fighting, mating, and the survival of the fittest. Like no name, he refused to die, and he refused to go away, despite the abuse the Brothers heaped upon him.

"To the Circle," the old one announced grandly, lapsing into another coughing spasm.

"Why bother?" asked no name, fully aware that the Brothers would not allow him to attend the Circle until he earned a name.

"The Brotherhood must be represented."

"Why?"

"We have interests in the Circle!" The old one's body lurched backward and he released a large, gooey brown mass from his mouth. The Brothers stared in dark wonderment at the sheer size of it.

"What interests? They don't do anything in the Circle."

"Fools!" growled Fat Face. "You understand nothing. They must welcome us. It is the law of the Circle. We go because it gives us pleasure to watch them cringe."

"Sometimes, in spite of themselves, they possess useful information," added Dog Chaser.

Rat Eater eyed his rival suspiciously. "We learned that the large prey were on the move and vulnerable because humans had destroyed their nesting places. Good Hunting!" snarled Rat Eater.

No name saw an opportunity to ingratiate himself with a powerful Brother. "Only the strongest and the bravest felines hunt the large prey."

Rat Eater's yellow eyes remained distant. "They are the only prey worthy of my skills." He was alert for any reaction from Fat Face. There was none.

The old one began to cough uncontrollably once again. He almost choked before he regurgitated another lumpy mass. This time the Brothers' only response was disgust.

Fat Face, Rat Eater, and Dog Chaser left for the Circle. Fat Face led the way. His Brothers followed to the right and to the left of his shoulders, maintaining equal position to each other. They were not prepared to challenge Fat Face's right to lead them, at least not tonight. No name followed some distance behind, trying desperately to keep pace with the others. He simply did not possess the stamina.

"Hey, Brothers, wait for me!"

"You are not a Brother. You have no name. Go back!" screamed Fat Face.

He cried out once again. "Slow down, would ya!"

"Go back!" commanded Fat Face.

However, no name continued his pursuit. Fat Face stopped and turned abruptly. He stiffened his body, flattened his ears, and brandished his tail aggressively from side to side.

No name struggled with his fear. Fat Face and the Brothers intimidated him at every opportunity. They showed no mercy when he dared to fight. Each time he promised himself he had surrendered for the last time. As he approached Fat Face and stared boldly into his menacing green eyes, he could feel the courage begin to drain from his body. He hoped desperately that the huge tom would look away. Fat Face uttered a series of cries that shattered what was left of his resolve. He closed his eyes in submission, cowered with shame, and slowly walked away. His tormentor lunged at him halfheartedly just to amuse himself, and no name sprang headlong into a full gallop.

Fat Face, Rat Eater, and Dog Chaser looked at one another with dark, laughing eyes and continued their journey. Rat Eater had observed every detail of the confrontation. He scrutinized Fat Face, alert for the first sign of weakness. He was prepared to challenge him, but only when he calculated he would be able to succeed. Rat Eater took few risks. He studied every situation thoroughly before taking action. He shielded his thoughts and turned his sharp pointed face toward Dog Chaser.

"Nothing to fear there . . . courage, but no cunning . . . risk taking for its own sake. He will destroy himself before long and sleep forever."

Dog Chaser slowed to a walk and sniffed the evening air. He signaled his companions. "Watch this!" He knew a medium- sized dog was approximately a half block away. The dog was let outside at the same time each evening. Dog Chaser delighted in terrorizing the poor creature. The three cats hid behind a hedge and waited. Eventually the dog trotted by at an easy pace. Dog Chaser watched him lift his leg to relieve himself.

"Disgusting habits! Disgusting creatures!" He prepared to attack, flattening his body, slinking along the hedge, scanning his surroundings for the most advantageous place from which to strike. The unsuspecting dog continued his nightly routine.

"Stupid, undignified creatures," thought Dog Chaser. "All that silly posturing and tail wagging for the humans."

Dog Chaser had spent his early life with a canine who always treated him kindly. He studied the creature thoroughly, despising it for its superior strength, contemptuous of any weakness. Later he was abandoned, turned feral, and used the knowledge he had gleaned from the experience to prey on any canine who was vulnerable. These escapades had begun as a pass-time. Now they were a need, the basis for his reputation with his peers.

Dog Chaser saw an upcoming break in the hedge and used the element of surprise to his advantage. He launched his body through the air from a crouched position, landing on his victim's hindquarters, plunging his sharp teeth and claws into the flesh of the terrified creature. The dog yelped, twisting and turning its body in a desperate attempt to free itself from the pain. Dog Chaser was jubilant, riding his screaming victim in triumph. He released several piercing shrieks to further terrorize the poor beast and heighten his own excitement. Finally he released his claws and jumped to the ground. The dog was so grateful to escape the pain, it shot forward at a full run. Dog Chaser immediately hid and ran triumphantly back to his Brothers. He waited for some show of approval from Fat Face or Rat Eater; he got none. The three tomcats merely continued their journey toward the Circle.

Chapter 17

Tosey stopped grooming her smooth, gray coat to listen to the apparent silence.

"Fat Face . . . Dog Chaser . . . Rat Eater . . . all traveling together. That can only mean one thing. They will visit the Circle tonight."

Tosey had lost track of time. There was little light where she slept. She spent her days in the garage while her human was away at work. She had plenty of food, water, and soft places to sleep, but she longed for blue skies and sunshine. Her human was later than usual, and Tosey waited impatiently. The woman would let her outdoors when she returned home. She would call her to come inside again just before dark. Most of the time, Tosey gladly answered the call.

The woman had adopted her from an animal shelter. Tosey would always remember the day the woman looked into her cage and spoke to her softly. Tosey was immediately drawn to her and reached her paw through the wire to touch the woman's hand. The cage door swung open, and after a brief transit in darkness, she was released into a new life.

Tosey's ears shot forward. She recognized the hum of the woman's automobile, the closing of the car door, the click of her heels up the stone path. She followed the sounds through the living room and down the hallway to the door leading into the garage. The wait seemed endless. Tosey meowed loudly to keep the woman's attention. She had learned how easily humans could be distracted. She finally squeezed through a barely opened door, and in perfect trust, allowed the woman to sweep her off the floor into her arms.

The woman held Tosey close, stroking her and speaking to her in a gentle, soothing voice. Tosey purred loudly in an extravagant display of appreciation. She enjoyed this daily ritual immensely, but the moment the woman put her down, she raced to the front door. Her human responded appropriately and granted Tosey a few hours of freedom to enjoy the smell and the feel of the earth around her.

Tosey wiled away the remaining hours of twilight, visiting her favorite haunts. When she was ready for a nap, she leaped from a high fence alongside a house into one of her most desirable retreats. A single room jutting out from the main building formed an accessible shelf beneath an overhang. She settled into this protected space, licked her tapered, white paws until they were spotlessly clean, and drifted into a light, pleasant sleep. She heard the familiar call at dark to return home. Tonight she chose not to respond. She slipped back into her dreams until her unerring instinct signaled her that it was time to leave for the Circle.

Tosey had a decision to make as she trotted along the city streets toward the meeting place. She had made an exciting discovery and was reluctant to share it. "Least of all," she thought, "with that arrogant, sharp-clawed feline who is almost purebred. Purebred, indeed!" Honey Bee and some of her sister felines tolerated Tosey in the Circle. They rejected her on the streets because they considered her different.

Tosey returned her thoughts to the problem at hand. She concluded it was just a matter of time before the others discovered her secret, so she might as well appear magnanimous. She comforted herself with the thought that Honey Bee might not attend the Circle that night.

Chapter 18

Honey Bee had passed the late afternoon in bored discontent. She paced from one favorite sleeping place to another, murmuring her displeasure in the sharp-edged voice typical of a Siamese. She also possessed the physique, seal-brown points, and abundant temperament of the breed. Four white paws and an odd splash of white across her muzzle betrayed her mixed origins. She watched a small, black poodle walk down a narrow hallway in her direction. She deliberately met him half way.

Honey Bee focused her power into her large blue eyes and glared at the poodle with genuine hostility. "Empty headed tail-wagger!" She seized every opportunity to humiliate him and had joyfully swiped him with her sharp claws more than once. The poor beast was anxious to escape her and trotted into the kitchen to seek human protection. She followed him, but allowed herself to be momentarily distracted by the contents of her dish. Her favorite treat did nothing to cure her ill humor. She finally jumped into an open, screened window and stretched her elegant body the length of the sill. She lay with her eyes half closed, waiting for the sky to totally darken around a dazzling full moon.

Honey Bee knew instinctively when it was time to leave for

the Circle. She jumped from the sill, touching the floor lightly, and trotted to her cat tree. She clawed vigorously at the carpeting for the health of her claws and to release some of her intense excitement. Her human was reluctant to let her out after dark, but Honey Bee was intelligent about getting her own way. Over time she had successfully conditioned her human. She approached the woman affectionately, brushing softly against her leg to get her attention, and uttering a series of loud, dissonant meows as a signal to let her outside. The woman did not respond.

"Dim-witted creatures!" thought Honey Bee. She gathered what little patience she possessed and trotted to the back door, reaching up to rattle the doorknob with her paw. The woman seemed to appreciate this intelligent display, but still did not respond appropriately.

Honey Bee narrowed her blue eyes and rapidly pushed three puffs of air through her nostrils in utter disdain. "Humans can be as dense as that pesky, mentally deficient canine I'm forced to endure, but," she reminded herself, "just as predictable." She retreated to the living room to consider her next stratagem.

Honey Bee unleashed a tremendous burst of energy. She dashed through the living room, skidding across the hardwood floors as she rounded the corner into the kitchen. She leapt from the floor, to the chair, to the sink, onto the forbidden table pausing with one foot on a dinner plate and another on a spoon to ensure her human would grab her and toss her outside. "There!" she thought. "That should do it!" The woman's voice was loud and harsh, but she took no action.

Honey Bee puffed several times in frustration. "Not quite angry enough." She walked with great dignity and deliberation to a large, overstuffed chair in the living room. She repeatedly sank her claws into the soft, thick upholstery and waited. She heard angry words, but nothing more.

Honey Bee was puzzled by her failure. She returned to the kitchen to gauge the effects of her tactics. The poodle observed her antics with smiling eyes from a safe spot under the kitchen table. His amusement infuriated her! "I could make you bleed, you silly beast! That always upsets her." She gave the poodle her most terrifying look. "One swipe of my paw and I know I would feel better!"

Honey Bee puffed arrogantly and isolated herself in the living room to consider her next move. "I must find a solution quickly," she thought, refusing to accept defeat. Her chilly blue eyes brightened with inspiration. "Ah, yes! My human is usually so responsive, I almost forgot. Well, I will give her one last chance."

Honey Bee wove in and out of the woman's legs, brushing against her with apparent affection, murmuring and meowing to be let outside. She stopped and waited. There was no response. "That does it!" She rubbed her head against the woman's ankle, searching for just the right spot, and sank her teeth into the bare skin. The woman cried out in astonishment and pain, grabbed Honey Bee, and threw her out the front door.

"Yeow!" screamed Honey Bee in delight as she triumphantly dashed into the night. "If all else fails, bite!" She bolted across the lawn onto the sidewalk with such speed she did not notice two other felines traveling in the same direction at a significantly slower pace.

Chapter 19

The meeting place for the Circle was some distance from the racetrack. Backstretch and Traveler stopped to rest and munched lazily on some grass growing near the sidewalk at the base of a large tree. Backstretch rolled energetically in the dirt and grass to smother as many fleas as possible. Traveler followed her example, covering his black coat with a blanket of gray dust.

Not too long ago, Traveler had prepared himself to die. Backstretch found him suffering from hunger, thirst, and exhaustion not far from the racetrack. Somehow he managed to follow her back to the tack room she shared occasionally with one of the grooms on shed row. Backstretch and the groom helped him to heal and to regain his strength.

Traveler was tempted to stay with Backstretch. He enjoyed her company and was curious about the mysteries of her way of life. However, he had been born and raised a Companion and fully intended to return to his former lifestyle. He had been accidentally separated from his human family and had already journeyed hundreds of miles with the complete trust that he would find them again. He was determined to resume his search as soon as he was fully recovered.

Meanwhile, Traveler spent his days with Backstretch, exchanging thoughts, and playing in nearby fields. He gained some understanding of what she called the Old Way. She had been born feral and was teaching him how to survive successfully on his own. He allowed her to absorb him into most of her daily routine, but was sometimes a reluctant participant.

Each day Backstretch visited the horses stabled along shed row. She loved the huge creatures and communicated with them as easily as she did with every bit of life around her. They terrified Traveler. Despite her constant reassurance, he did not trust them. Occasionally he trailed along behind her, ready to retreat in a heartbeat if one of the beasts snorted loudly or pawed nervously at its stable door.

Backstretch also attended a number of Circles on a regular basis. Traveler had never been to a feline gathering. He considered it unnatural for so many felines to congregate in one place at the same time. Tonight he had finally agreed to accompany her. However, he was adamant about one thing. He had learned it from his mother as a kitten. Felines should never climb trees. It was too dangerous and accomplished nothing.

Every day Traveler watched Backstretch shimmy up a tree, make her way skillfully through the branches, and remain above ground for hours. He watched her dig her claws into the bark, swing her body around, hanging fearlessly for a moment by her front claws, then catch the tree trunk with her back claws, and shimmy down again to a point where she could jump to the ground. Nevertheless, he would not consider spending any part of his day in a tree.

Backstretch understood. She loved her new friend and did not consider it her business to convince him of anything.

Backstretch was a Tree Climber and had been raised by the Strict Ones. She was comfortable perched high in a treetop surveying all that was above her and all that was below her. She looked forward to these hours alone, removed from all that was part of her normal routine.

The Strict Ones were Tree Climbers who lived in a closed community, avoiding human contact. They devoted themselves to preserving the purity of the Old Way, protecting their secrets, and passing them down through their generations. As Backstretch matured, she questioned their commitment to isolation, considering it an expression of fear contrary to the very truths she had been taught. She felt they concerned themselves with details that lost their importance from a high perspective. She believed wisdom should be shared freely with those who were ready to accept it.

Eventually, Backstretch made the painful decision to leave the community into which she had been born. The group did not prevent her departure, or forbid her return. However, her mother's farewell contained a warning: "Beware of the human. Learn from the plight of the canine. Never forget who you are. Never forget what it means to be feline."

Backstretch looked deep into Traveler's eyes with real affection. "Shall we continue?"

Traveler returned the gaze of the unusual creature before him. Her eyes shone with such light it was difficult to determine their color. Her coat was a swirl of white, black, gray, brown, and orange, as if she was something of everything. A compelling circle of white on her forehead was like an opening to new places, new experiences, new understandings.

Traveler wondered what further mysteries he would encounter this night. The prospect was exciting. The reality was strange and difficult to trust.

Chapter 20

The dark sky twinkled with light by the time Geraldine and her kittens finished eating and returned to the hilltop. The weather was mild, so they stretched out in front of the den.

Tiptoe contemplated the night sky, full of wonder. "Look at all of the tiny lights! How beautiful they are!"

Whisper agreed. "They sparkle like water drops in bright light."

Beetle stared at the night sky as well. He was dreaming his future.

Geraldine used this moment to tell her kittens about Lightfoot. She related what had happened to their friend as gently as possible.

"Won't we ever see Lightfoot again?" asked Beetle filled with deep sadness.

"He has separated from his body. It will sleep forever," explained Geraldine.

Whisper pressed deeper into his mother's soft fur. "If his body will sleep forever, where is Lightfoot?"

"I will tell you what I have been told. He has returned home."

"That's all?"

Tiptoe continued to gaze at the stars. "Where is home?"

"Where we began."

The kittens tried hard to understand.

"The Tree Climbers tell us our bodies are from this place. We are not."

"Really?" Tiptoe, Whisper, and Beetle wondered how this could be possible.

"Some things, little ones, can only be understood with the heart."

Geraldine and her kittens entered their den and snuggled close to one another, purring contentedly.

"My loves, I will visit the Circle tonight."

Beetle jumped to his feet in delight. "I am going too!" Before his mother could respond, he asked, "Will Fat Face be there?"

Whisper was equally excited. "I might see Father!"

"Maybe I will meet a Tree Climber! Oh! Are we old enough now?" asked Tiptoe.

It was difficult for Geraldine to disappoint them. "Tonight I must go alone."

"But, why?" insisted Whisper. His deep frustration surfaced in his compelling gold eyes.

Beetle looked at his brother with surprise. "Yes, why?" he added forcefully.

"You are not ready just yet to join the feline community. I will take all three of you to the Circle soon."

Tiptoe gave her mother a sullen look. "How soon?"

"My loves, please trust me a little bit longer to make this decision. There is still more you must learn."

Geraldine searched for a way to soften their disappointment. "When I return I will tell you who was there and describe everything that happened—every detail."

"Everything?" asked Whisper.

"Every detail?" asked Tiptoe.

"Promise?" asked Beetle.

"Everything. Every detail. I promise." Geraldine saw their eyes brighten.

"But now, you must each promise me something in return. You must remain in the den. There are dangers in the darkness you are not yet prepared to confront."

Tiptoe looked into her mother's eyes. "I promise."

"I promise," agreed Whisper.

"Me too," answered Beetle, a little too quickly.

Geraldine waited patiently.

"All right!" Beetle added reluctantly. "I promise."

Whisper gave his brother a forceful look that took Beetle by surprise. "We will remain in the den until you return. This time we will keep our promise."

"Come closer, little ones."

The kittens arranged themselves around their mother in a cozy half circle. Geraldine began to groom each one of them and, almost instantly, they were asleep. She waited for their sleep to deepen and slipped silently from the den.

Chapter 21

A few cloudy remnants strayed across the night sky momentarily dimming and then revealing a luminous, full moon. Geraldine traveled cautiously through the night, attentive to every detail of her surroundings. She sniffed the familiar markings of three dogs she had encountered in the area on prior occasions. She found no further sign of them.

Geraldine knew that she must see Romeo again, but her courage wavered as she drew close to the Circle. There were practical reasons for turning back. It was risky to travel far from her den late at night; she decided risk was a way of life for her now. Romeo might not attend; her inscrutable feline intuition assured her that he would be there. He might not be alone; she refused to believe that any of the females in the Circle could mean more to him than their friendship. She systematically dismissed each of her fears and continued her journey.

The Circle had already formed when Geraldine arrived. She hovered in the shadows, trying to summon the courage to join the other felines. All of the familiar faces were present, except Butterfly and Harmony. She saw Romeo immediately. He was lying much too close to an elegant female she did not recognize. She observed the stranger's remarkable symmetry and grace. She scrutinized every inch of her white satin coat, gleaming in the moonlight.

Geraldine's courage vanished. Tosey's casual remark and her meeting with Honey Bee returned to haunt her. Her feline pride would not allow her to approach Romeo looking less beautiful than when he last saw her. She decided to wait a few weeks and return when she regained her health and her appearance. However, it gave her such pleasure to watch him she could not bear to leave just yet.

Geraldine moved slowly along the ground trying to get as close as possible to the Circle. She nearly stumbled over a figure huddled in the tall grass. She was certain the creature was feline. Its lack of response puzzled her. When she realized the other cat was paralyzed with fright, she filled with compassion. She understood terror and loneliness. The stranger remained motionless, staring at her in total fear. Geraldine reclined slowly, facing the frightened stranger. Eventually she sensed the dark figure begin to relax.

"Please don't be afraid."

The stranger did not respond. It continued to stare wildly at her.

"I can help you."

There was still no response. Geraldine tried to coax the stranger toward the Circle.

"Follow me. The felines you have been watching will welcome you." Geraldine took a few steps forward and turned to look back. The stranger rose to its haunches.

"Come," Geraldine beckoned. "There is help in the Circle."

The cats in the Circle were totally absorbed in their own or one another's thoughts. They seemed unaware of Geraldine's approach or the shadowy figure lagging behind her. Geraldine took a deep breath and announced her arrival from an appropriate distance.

"I decided to join you."

Tosey was delighted. "How wonderful to see you!"

Geraldine gazed past Tosey, Romeo, and the gorgeous white creature next to him, forcing herself to continue calmly. "It is pleasant to be with you again."

Fat Face eyed her with the intense appreciation of a predator for its prey. However, felines did not attend the Circle to select mates. She ignored him, acknowledging Backstretch, Traveler, and finally, Raindrop.

"There are newcomers."

"Yes. One is a Tree Climber." Tosey turned toward Backstretch with respect. Fat Face and his Brothers sneered.

Geraldine knew instinctively that Backstretch was the Tree Climber. She was stunned by the appearance of the light around her body. It was broader and brighter than she had ever seen. The feel of it was different, more powerful than Romeo or Fat Face, with a warmth and gentleness beyond anything she had ever experienced. She studied the Tree Climber carefully, mesmerized by the sense of peace and joy she felt in her presence.

Geraldine filled with questions, but a faint, unfamiliar sound interrupted her thoughts and distracted the entire group. The sound moved steadily toward them. Every cat in the Circle watched the darkness, tense and expectant.

Moments later, a long haired, black female with white stockings trotted hesitantly toward the group, her movements punctuated by the rhythmic clap of a bell attached to her collar. Geraldine had forgotten the stranger she intended to introduce to the Circle. She rushed to her side to reassure her. The stranger scanned the Circle, looking for any sign of welcome. She chattered a variety of sounds, predominately "meow" in an effort to greet the others.

"Meow?" Honey Bee mimicked her sarcastically and puffed to express her indignation.

The stranger did not understand that felines reserved this greeting exclusively for humans. Her desperation momentarily neutralized her fear and she moved closer to the Circle.

"Ugh! Smells strange!" complained Honey Bee.

"Stop!" Geraldine defended the stranger. "I promised there would be help in the Circle. We were all strangers once. We discovered we shared more similarities than differences."

"The Circle is for everyone," Backstretch added softly.

Most of the cats purred loudly in unison to express their approval.

Dog Chaser ignored them. "That scent . . . neither male nor female . . . like . . ."

"Like me," interjected Tosey.

"And me," added Romeo. "This is common among us. There is no dishonor in it."

"None at all," Geraldine mused, withdrawing into secret thoughts. "You and I are both different now. Yet, nothing can change what I hold in my heart."

Fat Face glanced at Geraldine slyly and then scowled at Romeo. "Like you who would have us abandon the Old Way to seek human protection."

Romeo stood to address the accusation. "You and your Brothers do not live the Old Way." There was no anger in his expression. Conviction was the source of his strength. "This gathering is all that is left of the Old Way in your life or mine."

Tosey murmured her agreement. "We need humans now as much as they need us."

"Yes," agreed Backstretch. "That has always been true . . . true from the beginning for all things that live."

Fat Face had never vied with a Tree Climber. He was awed and challenged by the immense power he sensed in this smallish female. He kept his grudging respect expertly hidden. "Humans offer us nothing. We have always been the provider, not them."

Backstretch answered gently, "The Highest One is the only provider."

Fat Face's green eyes glittered with contempt. "Highest One? There is no Highest One!"

The confrontation terrified the bewildered stranger. She was afraid to leave and afraid to stay. She jumped closer to Geraldine for protection.

"What's that noise?" Honey Bee focused her attention on the stranger. "There! Again! Every time it moves."

"Obviously doesn't hunt," observed Rat Eater, matter-of-factly.

The stranger gave him an innocent, questioning look.

"Somebody do something about that noise—now!" Honey Bee scowled impatiently at Meow Baby. "You are difficult enough to accept. That noise is intolerable!"

"Your ill temper must be inbred," observed Romeo casually. "You never seem to be happy unless somebody else isn't."

"Ill temper indeed!" Honey Bee puffed several times in quick succession.

Geraldine could barely suppress her delight.

Tosey beckoned to Geraldine and the stranger. "Come, both of you, sit by me. How shall we address you?" she asked the stranger politely.

"I am called Meow Baby."

"Perfect!" exclaimed Honey Bee, with unmistakable sarcasm and four more puffs.

Meow Baby decided it was in her best interest to ignore Honey Bee and continue on. Her thoughts and feelings spilled from her so rapidly that even Honey Bee found it difficult to follow her story. "I am lonely, yes, lonely and hungry too, very hungry. I returned home again today. My human is not there. What will I do? Darkness has come and gone many times since she was taken away. She should have returned by now. I don't understand what has happened. Where could they have taken her? I just don't understand . . ."

"Sounds to me like you're homeless," interrupted Dog Chaser, forcing Meow Baby to pause and take a breath.

"Homeless? Me?" She paused again to consider this possibility. "Me? Homeless? No! Impossible! I know my human will return for me!"

Rat Eater observed the stranger coldly. "That's the way it is with humans. One day you're in, the next day you're out."

Geraldine felt old pain surface once again.

"Oh, no!" protested Meow Baby. "My human is devoted to me. We were inseparable."

Geraldine looked away. The stranger's story was similar to her own.

Meow Baby searched the faces of the other cats for understanding. "No! We were always together. She rarely left her sleeping place. I only left her side when it was absolutely necessary. But then they took her away."

Only Traveler would reassure her. "I was also left behind. I know in my heart it was a mistake and that my humans are as anxious to find me, as I am to find them. One day we will be reunited. I hope the same will be true for you."

"Yes. I must be patient. My human will return. But, how will I live? Where will I sleep? A feline like myself cannot beg or steal food. I am a Companion like my mother and her mother before her."

Geraldine thought of her kittens. Once there was security— even status—in being a Companion. "Tosey is right," she thought. "Life around us is changing."

"Oh yeah?" scoffed Rat Eater. "You'll beg and steal or you'll starve." He looked at his Brothers, mirroring the malevolent looks in their eyes.

"I can teach you to hunt," suggested Tosey with enthusiasm.

"Yes!" agreed Geraldine. "I learned from Tosey."

"Hunt? What is hunt?" asked Meow Baby.

"What? You can't be serious!" Honey Bee was amused and full of mischief.

Rat Eater sneered. "You won't teach that one to hunt. It has no claws."

Meow Baby was indignant. "I most certainly do!" But she referred to the claws on her hind feet. She had never had front claws within her memory.

Tosey and Geraldine looked down at Meow Baby's paws and back at each other in shock. Neither of them had ever encountered a feline without front claws.

"How can this be?" wondered Tosey. She immediately shielded her thoughts. She did not want to distress Meow Baby any further. "Pay no attention to them. We will find a way. But first we must do something about 'that noise.'" She stared accusingly at Honey Bee.

"Yes. Please do." Honey Bee puffed arrogantly.

"Oh, would you?" Meow Baby was clearly relieved. "It has always made me so . . . so . . . nervous."

"I understand," responded Tosey with kindness. She gently nuzzled Meow Baby's neck for evidence of the collar partially hidden in her thick, white ruff.

"Not that, too!" objected Meow Baby.

"It may be necessary."

"Never! It was my human's gift to me. I have worn it since . . . I can't remember. It is the symbol of our connection." A new sadness overwhelmed Meow Baby. "What will I do?"

Geraldine remembered that she still wore the collar the little human had placed around her neck.

"Gift?" Fat Face was livid. "You call that a gift? You willingly accept the canine stigma and consider it a gift?"

Fat Face raged at Meow Baby as she cowered between Tosey and Geraldine. He lived for these moments and glowered at her savagely to intensify her fear.

"Relax your big self before those cheeks burst! A collar can be a thing of great beauty." Honey Bee eyed the stones on Meow Baby's collar reflecting the moonlight. She imagined how lovely they would look gracing her own sleek, arched, exquisitely feline neck. "It's difficult to appreciate it half hidden on that insipid creature."

Geraldine jumped to her feet to defend her new friend. "Leave her alone—both of you!"

Tosey brushed her head tenderly against Meow Baby. "We have been through times like these. We survived with the help of the Great Mother. Trust in Her."

"What Great Mother?" Fat Face stood, raising his body to its full height. "It is my strength that I trust!"

"Intelligence!" declared Rat Eater.

"Courage!" argued Dog Chaser. "It is courage that will save you."

Backstretch reclined in front of Meow Baby. She extended her right front paw slowly and touched her gently. Meow Baby did not resist. The Tree Climber's touch was comforting, revitalizing, and renewed her hope, at least for the moment. Backstretch addressed her and the rest of the group:

"Most felines revere the source of all that exists. Some call it the Great Mother. Are you willing to think beyond feline?"

Meow Baby was more confused than ever. "Think beyond feline? What does that mean?"

"Please, just consider what I am about to tell you. It is time to expand our view of things. The source of all is not feline or canine, male or female. It is above us, below us, around us, in us . . . in everything that lives, supporting us every moment."

"Not feline? Not female? Everywhere? In everything?" Tosey was incredulous. "That cannot be! Why, many claim they have seen Her image in the High Place!"

"There are many images there. The Highest One embraces them all," explained Backstretch. "It is the source of what exists . . . the parent . . . we are the offspring."

"Then," concluded Raindrop, "we are all related."

Honey Bee jumped to her feet. "Surely this does not include . . . others . . . like the canine . . . or the human!"

"Yes, this includes all that lives."

"Do try to be discriminating! I'm not interested in being related to most felines, let alone some mangy canine or dull-witted human!"

"All related? Impossible!" roared Fat Face. "Tree Climber, you are a fool! Any feline who believes you is a greater fool!"

Raindrop glanced at Fat Face impatiently. "We are part of this Circle which expands each time we welcome a newcomer. Imagine a Circle like ours, but one so big it encompasses all that exists. It makes sense."

"Yes!" Romeo agreed with unconcealed admiration.

Geraldine's heart filled with envy. "It makes beautiful sense."

Fat Face chuckled inside at their gullibility. "Better for us," he thought. However, the mystery of the Tree Climber's power intrigued him. "Tree Climber, I want to see this 'Highest One' for myself—face to face."

"Then, look into the face of the feline next to you, or the human, or the canine, or . . ."

Fat Face glanced at Rat Eater to his right and Dog Chaser to his left and released a prolonged, searing hiss. "Nonsense!"

Meow Baby remained huddled between Tosey and Geraldine, terrified of what Fat Face and the Brothers might do next. She struggled to sustain the optimism she felt in the presence of Backstretch. Her fear was too great. Doubt and despair returned to torment her.

Chapter 22

Tosey decided this might be the opportune moment to reveal her recent discovery and free Meow Baby from the scrutiny of the group. She made the traditional, high-pitched sound to get the attention of the other cats. She kept her gaze unfocused as a show of respect.

Honey Bee refused to acknowledge her, deliberately distracting Raindrop and the felines near her. She swished her long tail mischievously. "What can she tell me that I need to know?"

Raindrop was curious. "Open your mind. We might learn something of interest." She turned her attention to Tosey.

"No malformed feline can tell me anything I don't already know!" She addressed Raindrop as if she were confiding a dreadful secret. "She has an extra toe."

"Really. What's wrong with having an extra toe?" Raindrop asked innocently.

Honey Bee had disliked Raindrop from the moment they met. She was intelligent, far too lovely, and truly a purebred. Now she disliked her even more. "Any feline who enjoys being wet and cold can't possibly understand."

"The scent and the feel of moisture falling gently from the High Place can be pleasurable," purred Raindrop.

The other cats winced at the thought.

Raindrop locked her patrician gaze on Honey Bee. "Perhaps the quality of my coat protects me from the unpleasantness you experience."

Honey Bee shot Raindrop a dark, intimidating glance to frighten her into submission. "Let me put it this way . . ."

"Of course."

"Do you know any felines with an extra toe?"

"No."

"Well?"

"So? I don't hear sound the way other felines do."

"What? You can't hear?"

"No. Yet you welcomed me . . ."

"And me," observed Backstretch, "and my friend who is a complete stranger."

"That was different. At least you look normal," she glared at Tosey, "and smell normal," she scowled at Meow Baby. "Even if that colorless feline enjoys being wet, and you waste your time sitting in those ragged green things. What do you do up there anyway? Sleep?" She uttered a low, derisive sound. "Take some advice. Find a place to sleep that's safer."

"A short fall is more dangerous for a feline than a fall from great height."

"Indeed!" Honey Bee puffed and looked away.

Raindrop could not resist. "How is it you failed to notice? I smell 'strange' too."

"Oh my—what else!" exclaimed Honey Bee.

Backstretch embraced the entire group with one sweeping glance, "The Circle is for everyone."

Geraldine addressed Backstretch with deep respect. "I know little about Tree Climbers and the Old Way. There is so much I want to know for my . . . for myself." She was careful not to mention her kittens in front of the Brotherhood. The females present, as well as Romeo, understood the unspoken danger and respected her privacy.

Geraldine asked Backstretch, "Will you teach me?"

"You already know more than you realize. You have simply forgotten. We all forget."

Geraldine paused to consider her next question. "Then, can you help me to . . . remember?"

"Are you seeking knowledge?"

"Yes. I am curious about your way of life. Tree Climbers live the Old Way and they are so wise."

"Then, is it wisdom you are really seeking?"

Geraldine thought for a moment. "Well . . . yes . . . it is."

"Wisdom is the birthright of any feline who desires it, not just Tree Climbers and those who live the Old Way. Seek the Highest One. Listen. When it is time, you will remember."

Geraldine felt drawn to the circle of white on the Tree Climber's forehead. For a moment she thought it glowed like a star in the night sky.

"It is time to lighten our lives with love."

"Pay attention to the Tree Climber," Romeo urged the group. "She sees life differently than most of us."

Raindrop tilted her beautiful face toward Romeo. "Differently?"

"More deeply . . . more clearly."

Rat Eater looked down his long, pointed nose at Romeo with complete contempt. "A feline who does not fend for himself, who does not reproduce his own kind, who no longer has the lust for a good fight is not entitled to an opinion."

Geraldine and the other cats waited anxiously for Romeo's response. He gave none.

Rat Eater continued. "The Tree Climber can't possibly see clearly from way up there. In my opinion she can't even see clearly down here!"

"I know felines who climbed trees and never saw anything at all," taunted Dog Chaser.

Backstretch returned to her original place in the Circle. "Perhaps their fear blinded them."

"Come down, Tree Climber! Join the rest of us. See life as it really is," jeered Rat Eater.

Backstretch studied Rat Eater with eyes that were open and loving. "Is it possible you are the one who cannot see?"

All of the felines present, except the Brotherhood, hummed their approval.

Romeo rose to his haunches to address the group: "There have been messengers like the Tree Climber throughout our history. Perhaps our task is not to credit or discredit the messenger, but to understand the message."

"And to live it," emphasized Backstretch. "Love is a way of life."

Romeo repeated the Tree Climber's thought with reverence. "And, to live it."

Geraldine could barely contain the pride and respect she felt for Romeo. She considered everything about him the epitome of feline.

Tosey had lost the attention of the group and waited patiently for an opportunity to rejoin the discussion. Rat Eater used her predicament to save face and change the subject. He turned toward her with a mock show of respect. "The feline with an extra toe had information to share with us before she was so rudely interrupted."

"Oh . . . well . . . yes." She began hesitantly, questioning whether she still wished to share anything with felines like Honey Bee and the Brotherhood.

"So, tell us!"

Tosey decided there was no point trying to keep a secret they would soon discover on their own.

"Well, there is a human a distance away who nurtures green creatures near her den. One of them is of particular interest to us." She sensed that she now had everyone's attention. Tosey added triumphantly, "the Pleasure Scent!"

"Where?" demanded Dog Chaser immediately.

"Yum!" Honey Bee was breathless. "This news is pure cream."

"Does the human share her den with any felines?" asked Raindrop, tantalized by the possibilities.

"Yes, but, they never leave the den."

"Captives!" snarled Fat Face. "Slaves to the human. Slaves to the Scent."

His hostility puzzled Tosey. She had expected the other cats to be delighted by her discovery.

"What's wrong with enjoying the Scent once in a while?" Dog Chaser's manner was charming, his aqua-colored eyes danced with anticipation.

"The Scent can make captivity more tolerable," agreed Raindrop.

Geraldine asked Backstretch: "What is your opinion?"

"The Scent is not the problem. It is our use of it . . . our reason for seeking it out. There are no answers in the Scent."

"It is the problem! The human uses the Scent to hold us captive—to steal our wildness from us," Fat Face argued in a blaze of temper. "Captives cannot understand what it means to be feline. Free felines need to be aware to survive."

"I agree that we must be aware to survive. However," Romeo challenged Fat Face once again, "are you suggesting that you and your Brothers are free and we are not?"

"Precisely!"

"Your message contains just enough truth to be deceptive. Your freedom is an illusion, Street Dweller. You are a scavenger who survives on whatever scraps the human leaves behind. You are as dependent upon humans as we are."

Fat Face curled his lip, hissed, and assumed a more aggressive posture. He and Romeo stared directly into each other's eyes.

Meow Baby's entire body began to tremble. Traveler was more convinced than ever that a feline gathering was a poor idea. Backstretch did her best to reassure both of them. Geraldine and the rest of the group were accustomed to these confrontations. They enjoyed the drama. They knew neither Romeo nor Fat Face would allow their disagreement to escalate any further. Challenges were acceptable in the Circle. The penalty for fighting was ostracism.

Dog Chaser broke the mounting tension. He was far more interested in the Pleasure Scent. "So, where is it?"

Fat Face seethed. "Only fools pursue the Scent!"

"It does no permanent harm. It merely enhances our pleasure."

"The world of sensation can overwhelm the sensitive, feline mind," warned Backstretch.

"Power is pleasure!" Fat Face showed his teeth. "Awareness gives power. Oblivion does not."

"Power?" Backstretch asked gently.

Fat Face focused all of his strength into his shallow green eyes, but could not force her to break eye contact.

"The greatest power," she continued, "is love."

"Love?" He was certain he had misunderstood her thought.

"Love?" Rat Eater's tiny eyes laughed at the idea.

"Yes . . . love . . . you know!" Dog Chaser was astonished his Brothers were so slow to comprehend the obvious.

Backstretch corrected him. "I am referring to love that extends beyond physical union, beyond ourselves and other felines, to everything that is."

There was a moment of light in Dog Chaser's eyes, but he had no desire to understand.

Backstretch continued, "When we choose to live in love we begin to fit the small pictures in our minds into the bigger picture that includes all that is. We benefit ourselves and everything around us."

Dog Chaser was uninterested. "A new kind of love. So what? Love comes, love goes . . . like everything else."

"The Highest One is unfailing."

"Power. Love. Highest One. Who cares?" Dog Chaser's eyes

glittered playfully. "I choose pleasure. Where do I find the Scent?"

"I will show you," answered Tosey, "but, we must be discreet and leave no trace of our visits."

"Pleasure! Comfort!" Fat Face flew into another rage. "The great seducers!" His celebrated cheeks seemed to grow even larger. "Have your feline comforts. Deface yourself with the canine stigma. I want none of it!"

Chapter 23

The attention of the cats shifted abruptly. Two more felines announced their arrival. The group opened the Circle to make room for Butterfly and Harmony. The latecomers greeted the others enthusiastically, acknowledged Traveler, and gave Meow Baby their complete acceptance. Geraldine was relieved to feel her anxious friend begin to relax again. "Love does make everything easier," she thought happily.

Honey Bee considered the arrival of Butterfly and Harmony a welcome diversion and managed a veneer of warmth. "So, the two of you managed to outsmart your human tonight. Good to see you. You visit so seldom."

"We have total freedom now," announced Butterfly grandly.

This news was unbearable. Honey Bee could barely tolerate the sound of Harmony's purr, and she had always resented Butterfly's superior athletic skills. She refused to befriend a feline who was able to jump higher than she could. Honey Bee unsheathed her claws. "What happened? Did she abandon you?"

"Of course not! Our human created a special opening from the interior of her den to the outside . . ."

"Just for us!" added Harmony proudly. "We can come and go as we please."

The other Companions were quite impressed. Honey Bee was furious. She could not imagine two more undeserving felines.

"Well," Honey Bee interjected casually, "if you can go in and out of this opening as you please, it seems to me that any creature your size can do the same . . . a small canine perhaps."

Butterfly was unconcerned. "We have considered that possibility. We are prepared."

"We work together," Harmony assured her. "The beast will wish he never entered our den."

"I see. Well," purred Honey Bee, "what about the fierce creature with the black eyes?"

"That creature does not travel through our territory," Butterfly answered confidently.

"Oh, didn't you know? They are everywhere nowadays."

"Really?"

"Oh, yes. And when they are cornered, I hear they can be ferocious!"

Butterfly and Harmony looked at each other anxiously. "May the Great Mother protect us!" they exclaimed in unison.

"Indeed." Honey Bee delighted in their fear and felt instant relief. She had succeeded in dulling the luster surrounding them and their good fortune.

Backstretch interrupted, "You must hear about Traveler's adventures. He has wonderful stories to tell."

Butterfly and Harmony's concern vanished with the promise of a good story. They pleaded with him to share his life history with the group. Traveler was relieved to limit his interaction with the other felines to storytelling. He began his tale, and every cat in the Circle, including Honey Bee, listened with rapt attention.

Geraldine tried to concentrate, but she gradually drifted to another place, the place where memories are kept. She had never stopped observing Romeo. She shielded her thoughts and experienced again the exquisite pleasure and the pain of their past together. Feline etiquette required her to renew their friendship. "Does he remember?" she wondered. "Will he leave Raindrop to accept a place beside me in the Circle?" She saw that Romeo was watching her.

"A canine helped you?" Dog Chaser's impassioned response to Traveler's story jolted Geraldine from her reverie.

"Spare me," muttered Honey Bee.

"Many of their kind have helped me along the way."

Romeo understood that a dog could also be a friend. "I share my den with a large white canine. We have always been close companions."

Butterfly and Harmony looked at each other in horror.

Dog Chaser knew that Romeo was truthful. However, it did not suit his purpose to admit that any canine possessed a single redeeming quality. "They are such vile, disgusting creatures— definitely inferior—undeserving of any respect."

"Well, I am forced to share my den with a small black canine." Honey Bee puffed insolently. "I only tolerate his presence because he is so easy to control. He doesn't know how to do anything but obey."

"The defect is inborn," explained Dog Chaser with contempt. "The canine has no life of its own. It exists to do the master's bidding."

Fat Face and Rat Eater agreed, acknowledging Dog Chaser's expertise in this matter.

"Ah, yes." Honey Bee's oval blue eyes glittered in the moonlight. "Humans cherish obedience. They apparently consider it a sign of intelligence. Can you imagine? One evening I observed a particularly disgusting display."

"What happened?" asked Butterfly. She was not fond of Honey Bee, but she had to admit she found her stories entertaining.

"The human ordered the canine to sit." Honey Bee shuddered melodramatically at the memory.

"Oh, my," mewed Raindrop. "Did it obey?"

"Of course. What did you expect? Next, the human placed food on his muzzle."

The other cats looked at one another quizzically, unable to comprehend why the human would do such a meaningless thing.

"But, why?" asked Butterfly.

"Power." Backstretch gave Honey Bee and the members of the Brotherhood a long, searching look. "Until we find our own power, we prove our strength by stealing it from others."

"Will you please allow me to finish my story?" Honey Bee paused dramatically, feigning insult. "Thank you! Well . . . where was I? To continue . . . the witless creature plainly wanted the food."

"So, what happened?" Butterfly was bursting with curiosity.

"Prepare yourself for this one."

"Yes! Yes!" Butterfly grew impatient. "Tell us what happened next."

"He sat there balancing it on his muzzle . . ."

"That should have been easy enough for him to do."

"Would you stop interrupting and let me finish?"

"They perform for the human, you know."

"*Great Mother of Cats!*" Honey Bee struggled to keep her temper. Butterfly gasped, unaccustomed to such blasphemy.

"*Can I finish now?*" Honey Bee gave Butterfly the most menacing look in her repertoire.

"Why, yes . . . yes . . . of course."

"Well, he sat there balancing it on his muzzle until . . ." she paused again . . . "until the human gave him *permission* to eat it!"

"No!" protested Tosey.

"Can this be true?" questioned Harmony.

Geraldine also found this difficult to believe. "Really?"

"How . . . degrading!" exclaimed Raindrop.

"And, for what?" continued Honey Bee.

"For approval," answered Fat Face immediately. "This need runs deep in the canine."

"And the ignorant beast got it!" Honey Bee's icy blue eyes darkened with jealousy.

Romeo felt he could help the others understand. "My canine friend tells me that his kind used to live in groups like humans and follow a leader. We felines are simply different. Although some choose to live in communities . . . like humans," he glanced at Fat Face and the members of the Brotherhood, "we are, for the most part, solitary creatures and follow no one."

Fat Face reacted immediately. "A true feline obeys no one. A true feline serves no one. A true feline . . ."

Backstretch finished his thought, " . . . follows his or her own heart." She bowed her head humbly to purrs of approval.

"Well, we are definitely the only creatures capable of such noble behavior," concluded Honey Bee.

Backstretch disagreed. "Not at all. Nobility can be found in the canine, the human . . . in all creatures."

"Indeed!" Honey Bee jerked her tail back and forth energetically to express her intense irritation at Backstretch. She could not unleash her anger in her preferred manner without risking ostracism. "It is common knowledge that canines are lesser creatures. The vibrations from their bodies are . . . dense."

Fat Face agreed. "Like humans."

"There are dense vibrations around any creature who lives in fear," Backstretch answered calmly.

Honey Bee addressed the group: "If any of you have ever tried to communicate with a human or with a canine, even the most patient among us," she glanced pointedly at Backstretch, "must admit it is next to impossible. They are *dense!*"

"A loving heart will enable you to communicate with any creature you wish."

"My feline intelligence, you mean!"

"I mean love," insisted Backstretch. "The invisible link between felines exists among all those who love."

"Love . . . again!" Honey Bee puffed.

"It is the most powerful force, the only source of true strength."

"The Brotherhood understands strength!" Fat Face roared. "We have no need for love."

Honey Bee looked at Backstretch and arched her neck arrogantly. "I will gladly minimize my need to communicate with non-felines, so I don't need it either."

"Strength!" growled Fat Face.

"Intelligence!" exclaimed Rat Eater.

"Courage!" declared Dog Chaser. "These are essential for survival."

"Admirable qualities," admitted Backstretch, "but easily misplaced. Without love they can bring chaos, breakdown . . . much heartache."

Suddenly, Geraldine felt that Backstretch was addressing her personally. "Faith gives love a safe place to grow. Faith will save a feline in the face of the impossible."

"Never forget beauty," Romeo reminded the group. "Felines must have beauty in their lives to survive."

"Yes. Beauty," agreed Dog Chaser.

"Only if they are weak," hissed Fat Face.

Geraldine watched Romeo and Raindrop. She thought they must be the most beautiful felines she had ever seen. She felt farther away from Romeo than ever.

Backstretch glanced around the Circle quickly. "Beauty is everywhere."

She reclined sphinx-like in the center of the Circle. "Change is coming."

"Change? Oh, no!" exclaimed Meow Baby, horrified at the thought of another calamity in her life.

"What change?" asked Geraldine calmly.

"What we have learned through the generations will now come together in a different way. Many will perceive alternatives to the old way of being. Many will choose love rather than fear, peace rather than conflict."

"What?" Fat Face exploded. "No conflict? No struggle? No triumph? This cannot be! Why continue?"

"Must you have strife to convince yourself you are alive? There is another way."

"Not for me! Not for the Brotherhood! We will never be a part of this!"

"We are always free to choose. Happiness is everywhere. Sadness is everywhere."

"If it's peace you want, simply eliminate the canine," suggested Dog Chaser, his intense aqua eyes full of humor. "Then you will have peace."

"Or perhaps the human . . . they bring nothing but trouble," proposed Rat Eater, amused by the thought.

Tosey rose to her feet. "If felines were in charge, we would all be better off."

The other cats purred loudly to express their agreement.

"True, lasting peace," explained Backstretch, "begins within each of us. It is achieved from the inside out—not by eliminating outside influences. The solution is to become masters of ourselves, not others."

Backstretch turned within for a moment. Geraldine felt the light around the Tree Climber's body grow in size and intensity, filling the Circle with warmth and love, gifted freely to any feline who wished to accept it.

Geraldine's ears shot forward in response to a muffled, anguished cry in the distance. "That sound was feline!"

"Yes, yes," Honey Bee answered impatiently. "Ignore it. We always do."

"I will do no such thing!" Geraldine protested, sensing a feline in distress.

"Unfortunately," lamented Honey Bee, "any feline who wants to join us can walk into the Circle . . . just like your new friend here."

"He dared to follow again!" Fat Face gave his Brothers a dark look.

"Who?" inquired Backstretch.

"Do not concern yourself. He has no name."

"Impossible! All felines have a name."

Fat Face dismissed her objection. "You must earn your name in the Brotherhood."

Dog Chaser repeated, "He has no name."

The Tree Climber rose to leave the Circle. "If this feline wants help, we will return together. The Circle is for everyone."

Backstretch found no name hiding in a thick patch of weeds.

"Join us if you wish."

"Go away!" he hissed.

She ignored his hostility.

His manner became more threatening. "Go away!"

"Do you really want me to leave?"

"Do the Brothers know I am here?"

"Yes."

"Thanks to you, they may kill me this time."

"No harm will befall you in the Circle."

"Afterwards," he scowled, "they may kill me."

"And they may not."

"Who are you?"

"A friend."

"To me? Nobody is my friend."

Backstretch remained steadfast.

His belligerence turned to pleading. "Please go away. They'll just hurt me again . . . bad . . . and hurt you too. I'm not worth it. Leave me alone."

"You are worth it."

A mix of curiosity and shattered hope gave no name enough strength to look into the eyes of the Tree Climber. He felt the impulse to trust for the first time within his memory.

"Will you walk with me?" she asked.

"You'll be sorry. We'll both be sorry."

"I'm willing to risk it."

Backstretch turned to go back to the Circle. She heard hesitant footsteps.

"Are you coming?"

"Wait!" he cried out. "Why are you doing this? I'm nobody." He admitted the depth of his disgrace, convinced she would abandon him. "I have no name."

"Who are you?" she asked gently.

"I told you." He hung his head in shame. "Nobody . . . nothing."

"That is a lie."

Backstretch rejoined the Circle with no name at her side. She offered him a place between Romeo and herself. No name crouched low, ears flat against his head, his eyes averted as if he could make himself invisible.

Fat Face ordered his Brothers, "Look the other way—for now."

Most of the felines found it difficult to look at no name at all. Poor grooming was most unfeline. They considered Fat Face, Rat Eater, and Dog Chaser unkempt, but they wore their scarred, rumpled coats with pride as a symbol of their prowess and courage. No name was just disheveled.

"More feline riff-raff," muttered Honey Bee. "First that one," she indicated Meow Baby, "and now this."

Raindrop enjoyed reminding her, "The Circle is for everyone."

Backstretch regained the attention of the group and most of the felines quickly forgot about the presence of no name.

"Yes, there will be great change," she continued. "It is not an accident that felines are replacing canines as the human's preferred companion."

"I already have!" Honey Bee puffed impatiently. "So what?"

"They have learned much from their long association with the canine. They will learn new things from us."

Raindrop stared at Backstretch thoughtfully. "Humans . . . learn from us? How? What must we do?"

"Just be feline. The best teaching is by example."

"The only way to teach humans is through exhausting effort," snapped Honey Bee. "They are not only *dense*, all they care about is themselves."

"You, like many felines, manipulate humans to get what you want."

"Of course I do."

"Manipulation requires a lot of energy."

"I must look out for myself." Honey Bee puffed, gave Backstretch an irritated look, and puffed again. "What's wrong with that? I look out for myself. They look out for themselves."

"We can look out for others as well as for ourselves."

"I could, but I won't, my sage friend. I like things just the way they are. My way!"

Raindrop continued to focus on the possibility of teaching by example. Her pale blue eyes filled with enthusiasm. "I understand. Flexibility is our strength . . . and balance . . . and . . ."

"Yes." Geraldine also understood. "We know the importance of quiet and rest. Humans surround themselves with endless streams of sound. They are constantly running here and there. They are always busy."

Backstretch continued, "Few humans take time to listen to their hearts."

"Or allow themselves to appreciate the extraordinary beauty around them," added Romeo. "Do they watch the High Place gradually darken to reveal its hidden treasures or observe a moonrise slowly illuminate the darkness with its soft glow?"

Geraldine was taken by surprise. She busied herself grooming her coat to conceal her deep-felt response to the pictures in her mind.

"Do what?" asked Meow Baby.

"Not my human," answered Tosey.

"Nor mine," agreed Raindrop sympathetically.

"How can they? Humans spend most of their time shut away in one den or another," observed Romeo.

Tosey was skeptical. "Do you really believe we can slow them down?"

Honey Bee already considered herself an expert at interrupting humans at work. "Trust me. I do it all the time."

"Remember," Backstretch cautioned, "we can also learn from them."

Fat Face roared again. "Beware! Felines who choose to live with the human will suffer the fate of the canine. See how thoroughly this ... this ... Meow Baby has adapted to human ways."

"Human contact has brought change," Romeo stated boldly. "We must change."

"Learn from the human." Backstretch repeated her mother's warning: "'Never forget who you are. Never forget what it means to be feline.'"

Rat Eater could no longer remain aloof. "Surely you don't believe all this nonsense?" He crept toward Backstretch in a slow, intimidating manner. "You are a perfect example of what happens to felines who climb trees indiscriminately. The experience distorts your perceptions. Now you wish to distort ours as well."

"Everything around us looks different from a higher place."

"Can we please move on?" Honey Bee was impatient to change the subject. "I come to the Circle to relax and enjoy myself. This profound exchange has become quite boring. Traveler, tell us more about your journeys. At least you are clever enough to be entertaining."

Traveler was happy to resume his tale.

Chapter 24

Once again, Geraldine's thoughts wandered from Traveler to Backstretch, and eventually to Romeo. She secretly glanced in his direction from time to time, still tangled in indecision. The past was no more. The future was a mystery. Perhaps there would be other nights and other Circles, perhaps not. She could feel him also watching her.

Finally, the strength of Geraldine's love freed her to live this moment and follow her heart. She deliberately met Romeo's gaze, allowing all of the love she felt for him to light her lovely green eyes. His response was immediate. He welcomed her into his thoughts and walked slowly toward her.

Traveler was deep into his story. The other cats listened intently. They were also keenly aware of the interaction between Romeo and Geraldine.

Although Geraldine had dreamed this scene many times, it was difficult for her to believe it was really happening. Romeo reclined gracefully beside her. According to custom, she lowered her head, permitting him to gently groom her crown and her forehead. Her memories had not betrayed her. Romeo's nearness was as comforting to her now as it had been in the past.

Just as suddenly as the moment began, it ended. Geraldine and Romeo had satisfied feline etiquette. They had acknowledged the renewal of their friendship to each other and to the Circle. He rose and returned to his place next to Raindrop.

"Oh!" Butterfly and Harmony both uttered heartfelt sighs. Tosey and Raindrop were equally moved. Most felines, with the exception of the Brotherhood, considered it a privilege to witness this traditional ritual. However, Honey Bee could only envy the beauty of a committed heart.

The Circle now gave their complete attention to Traveler and the story he was telling. Geraldine was finally at peace. She was able to listen to Traveler with genuine interest until she heard Meow Baby move. Meow Baby immediately froze to silence the bell on her collar, terrified of another confrontation with Honey Bee.

Geraldine was concerned about the fate of her new friend. She withdrew her thoughts from the rest of the group and considered whether any of the problems Meow Baby faced could be solved before the group disbanded. She glanced up at the position of the moon and realized there was little time left.

Geraldine doubted that Meow Baby would ever learn to hunt efficiently without front claws. Even if she did, it would take time. She remembered that she almost starved while she learned. She considered bringing her back to her den, but promptly dismissed the idea. "There must be a way." Geraldine deepened her concentration. She rose suddenly, assured Meow Baby and Tosey that she would return, and politely excused herself from the Circle.

Traveler completed his tale, and the group fell silent. The full moon had moved across the sky to the place that signaled the cats to disband. Backstretch had reintroduced an ancient practice at the close of each gathering. The custom had been lost to most Companions and Street Dwellers through the generations.

The Brotherhood considered the practice useless. Fat Face, Rat Eater, and Dog Chaser left abruptly to return to their sleeping places. Before their departure, Fat Face gave no name a final, devastating look. "We'll deal with you later." No name hugged the ground, desperate to find a way to postpone the inevitable. Honey Bee had no desire to leave until she satisfied her curiosity about Geraldine's whereabouts. Meow Baby stayed close to Tosey. The other felines had experienced the value of this practice and were eager to follow the Tree Climber's instructions.

Backstretch began to explain. "We have all basked in the warm light, relaxing every muscle in our bodies."

Meow Baby remembered stretching out on a long table, luxuriating in the late afternoon sunshine. She sighed, re-experiencing that feeling of prolonged relaxation, her every want, her every need satisfied.

"Yes, I understand."

Backstretch continued, "When you hunt . . ."

"Hunt . . . again!" Meow Baby interrupted anxiously. "But I don't understand 'hunt.'"

"Calm yourself, my friend." Tosey pressed her head against Meow Baby's shoulder. "You will learn soon."

Backstretch continued to explain. "When you hunt, you must be so still you become one with all that surrounds you. This requires intense concentration. Your focus is your prey. We will change the focus and use this skill in a different way. Allow yourself to relax and we will travel to that same, still place together."

Geraldine reappeared suddenly and announced her arrival.

"I have brought our new friend a gift." Geraldine dropped something from her mouth just outside the perimeter of the Circle near Tosey and Meow Baby. Meow Baby looked at the gift, at Tosey, and back to Geraldine.

"What is that?"

"It is food to ease your hunger."

"Am I supposed to eat . . . that?"

Geraldine was thankful for the experience she had with her kittens. "Yes, my friend, sometimes it is necessary. This is why we hunt." Geraldine leaned over the dead mouse and began to eat. "Will you join me?"

"Yes," Tosey encouraged her, "go ahead. It is nourishing."

"Was this once a creature with life?"

"Yes."

Meow Baby looked at Geraldine sadly. "Must I . . . hunt in order to survive?"

"There are alternatives," answered Backstretch, "if you wish to explore them."

Although Meow Baby was reluctant, she was also hungry. She followed Geraldine's example. She ate slowly at first, but soon adapted to this new experience.

"Oh, thank you. I did not mean to be ungrateful. This is just so strange to me."

Geraldine noticed for the first time that the Brotherhood had left the Circle early. She allowed a twinge of fear to pass quickly. She took thorough precautions every day to protect the location of her den from all predators. More important, she felt assured at a deeper level that they posed no threat on this occasion, at least not to her or her kittens.

As soon as Meow Baby had finished, Backstretch began her explanation again.

"Do you have to start from the beginning?" complained Honey Bee. "We know that already."

Backstretch ignored her. She patiently retraced her thoughts until she reached the point where Geraldine had returned. "Now, allow yourselves to relax and be still."

"Just focus on the sound of your purr," suggested Harmony, trying to be helpful. "You'll find it makes it easier for you to relax."

That was more than Honey Bee could endure. "*Great Mother of Cats!* Are you serious? How are we supposed to do that with you here?"

Harmony was bewildered. "I don't understand."

"Well, if your best friend won't tell you, I will!"

Butterfly intervened. "You . . . stink . . ."

"Oh my!" interrupted Harmony, determined to prevent an irreversible confrontation.

Butterfly was grateful for a moment to rethink her initial response. Instead she gave Honey Bee a burning look. "Do us all a favor and keep your thoughts to yourself."

"Indeed!"

Meow Baby studied Honey Bee with honest, searching eyes. She asked quite innocently, "Why are you so mean?"

Honey Bee was dumbstruck. "You . . . you . . . you . . ." She fumbled for a sufficiently scathing response, but had none. She finally settled for, "How dare you!"

The other cats exchanged quick, sidelong glances, relishing Honey Bee's unusual predicament. However, Meow Baby was trembling again. "I'm . . . I'm sorry," she stammered. She looked to Tosey and Geraldine for reassurance. "Did I do something wrong?"

Geraldine leaned closer to Meow Baby, "Not a thing, sweet friend. Just calm yourself and listen to the Tree Climber." She looked squarely at Honey Bee. "The right question can be disarming."

Backstretch seized the moment to begin her explanation once again. Most of the group allowed her to guide them. They permitted deep serenity to replace any anxiety they carried in their bodies and released a rich chorus of resonant purrs into the night. The collective sound exerted a pleasant, hypnotic effect on the group, with one exception. Honey Bee remained hopelessly fixated on the atonal sound of Harmony's purr.

"Ridiculous," she thought, as she looked at the peaceful, contented faces around her. "What they don't hear can't irritate them." Honey Bee congratulated herself on the superiority of her heightened feline senses, and with one final puff, strutted into the darkness.

Sometime later, the cats in the Circle became active again. Geraldine raised her body to a sitting position and noticed that the nagging pain in her right shoulder was gone. She kept moving her shoulder to convince herself the discomfort had actually disappeared. She was also aware of renewed physical energy and mental clarity that translated into a general feeling of well being.

Butterfly watched her closely. "You feel different, don't you?"

"Oh, yes!" Geraldine exclaimed joyfully. She glowed with new energy and, like the others, attributed the experience to Backstretch.

"You may each experience something different," Backstretch reminded them. "These are your experiences, not mine. They are quite personal and have always been deep inside you waiting to be tapped. I have merely helped you to remember how to access them."

Geraldine studied the strange circle of white on Backstretch's forehead. "My little ones are too young to bring to the Circle. I want them to learn from you. Will you visit our den?"

Backstretch looked at Geraldine as if she were searching every part of her. "When the time is right, I will come." She turned her attention to no name. "If you wish, you can come with Traveler and me."

"I don't know what to do. If I go back, they'll probably kill me. If I go with you, I don't know what will happen."

"Can the unknown be any worse than what you already know?"

No name did not respond.

"There is a place where you can regain your physical strength. We will be forced to move soon. Too many humans leave their unwanted felines there. The area can no longer support our population."

"Regain my physical strength? That's impossible."

"My friend, Traveler, will assure you that it is not."

"You mean I can be strong?" He thought for a moment. "Then I'll make them sorry. I'll beat them up . . . make them cower . . . watch them grovel. Yes," he decided, "I'm going with you."

"If that's what you want, go back to them! If you want to explore a different way, come with me."

"A different way? Well, at least I'd never have to deal with them again."

"Make no mistake. You must reclaim more than your physical vitality. To find your true strength, you must face them again. But it is yourself you must master—not them."

"Is that possible?"

"You decide."

Traveler joined Backstretch to begin their long journey to the racetrack. He walked away from the Circle convinced, beyond a shadow of a doubt, that he preferred the company of humans. Backstretch turned to the rest of the group. "Farewell! Seek the Highest One from the inside out." She looked over her shoulder one last time. "Fall into love and live there!"

"Wait! Wait for me!" No name scampered after them.

The remaining cats watched respectfully until the Tree Climber and her companions disappeared from sight.

Butterfly and Harmony prepared to leave. "Our new freedom will permit us to visit the Circle more often. Will we see you again soon?" Butterfly asked Geraldine.

"Yes."

"Wonderful! Until then, may the Great Mother protect you . . . or is it the Highest One? What did the Tree Climber tell us? Oh, my! So many new ideas . . ."

"So confusing." Harmony remained skeptical. "I'm not sure what to make of this new . . . or is it really old knowledge? Whatever! Farewell!"

Geraldine turned to her friend Tosey with deep affection. "I am so pleased I came to the Circle tonight. I needed your encouragement." She and Tosey touched noses, purring softly. Suddenly they realized they had both forgotten about their new friend. Meow Baby sat beside them, anxiously watching the other cats leave the Circle.

Her large eyes filled with fear. "What am I to do?"

Tosey observed Meow Baby a few minutes longer and made her decision. "Come with me, my friend."

"I can't," Meow Baby replied sadly. "What if my human returns and I am not there?"

Tosey did her best to comfort Meow Baby and told her what she felt was the truth. "I do not believe your human will return. I believe she was taken away to sleep forever."

"No!" protested Meow Baby. "That can't be!"

Tosey continued gently. "You must come with me. I know a place where you will be safe. Soon you will be hungry again . . . and thirsty . . . and cold. Perhaps my human will help."

Meow Baby chose reluctantly to follow Tosey into the night.

Geraldine was relieved. At least Meow Baby, like no name, would be safe for the time being. Geraldine said goodbye to Romeo and Raindrop and watched them leave together.

She lingered a while longer, and then left as she had arrived, alone.

Chapter 25

Geraldine's heart radiated joy. She had made peace with her past. She was at peace in the present. Geraldine felt as clear and fresh on the inside as the air she breathed in around her. Her paws barely touched the ground as she trotted happily toward home. She was alert as always, but her body seemed lighter and danger seemed less real to her now.

Although Geraldine was eager to curl up with her kittens and keep her promise to share every detail of the evening, her heart insisted on one final visit to complete this night. She mentally nuzzled Tiptoe, Beetle, and Whisper. Her deep maternal Knowing assured her that they had kept their promise and were sleeping peacefully in the den.

Geraldine sprinted down a driveway and jumped to the top of a gate, balancing there for a moment to gaze reverently at the garden. She opened her heart freely to its sacred beauty and to the memories she had shared with Romeo. Their garden was different now, as one season lingered and another began, but to Geraldine, it had never been lovelier. The moon glow was as soft as candlelight. The spring flowers had finished their work and dozens of rose bushes yielded a splurge of dazzling, new color. One bush in particular attracted her attention. The energy around it drew her closer. The leaves were dark, vibrant green. The tall, straight stems, bursting with opalescent white blossoms, reached for the stars. And there, sitting beneath the rose bush, like a vision in the moonlight, was Romeo.

"Over here!" he called to her in his deep, musical voice.

Geraldine turned her head away and then looked back again slowly to be certain her eyes had not betrayed her.

"Here!" he called again.

She floated toward the vision. When Romeo touched her nose gently in greeting, she finally believed that her deepest wish had come true. He invited her to inhale the fragrance of a magnificent white rose unfolding from its center. "I sensed that you would come."

Geraldine savored its delicate perfume, and the two of them wandered joyfully from one rose bush to another, totally immersed in each other and in the beauty around them.

Romeo and Geraldine jumped onto the ledge surrounding the pond to watch the brightly colored fish ripple the surface as they swam for the protection of the water plants. When the surface calmed, they stared with delight at their shadowy image and the wavering reflection of the full moon. They followed their familiar path through the gazebo and lay side by side on the plush, damp lawn. Their thoughts flowed together effortlessly, as in all genuine friendships.

Romeo drew closer to Geraldine in the moonlight. "I remember the first time I saw you."

Geraldine lowered her head apologetically. "I have changed so much."

"We have both changed."

She could not resist asking, "What do you remember?"

"Everything."

Geraldine brushed Romeo's nose softly, feeling light and buoyant again. She realized she had worried about things that did not matter. They had always been friends first.

Romeo watched her carefully. "You have small ones now."

"I want you to know them. Soon they will be old enough."

Geraldine felt his tenderness surround and embrace her. She realized she had almost permitted fear to deny her the experience of this wonderful night. "Yes," she thought. "Happiness is everywhere. Sadness is everywhere. We choose love or we choose fear."

Romeo answered her thought. "The Tree Climber is wise. Love can make our dreams come true. Fear can destroy them."

Eventually it was time for them to leave their enchanted world. Their delight in this place was interwoven with their deep affection for each other. They knew they would always return here to cherish the past and to dream the future.

Romeo joined Geraldine for part of her trip home. They trotted along the streets together in high spirits, stopping here and there in the shadows just to be close. A strange night sound provided an excuse to dart down a driveway and seek shelter in a fragrant cluster of lilacs. There was no real danger. They lingered a few moments, shielded from the outside world, soothed by each other's presence, comforted by the sweet fragrance and the smell of damp earth. When they finally reached the end of their dreamlike journey, they touched noses affectionately and vowed to meet again soon.

Geraldine's eyes sparkled with the love and respect she felt for Romeo. "I will miss you."

He nuzzled her cheek softly in the final, tender moment before parting. "I am always close to you. We are joined at the heart."

Romeo and Geraldine turned away from each other and stepped back into reality. Their world changed in the twinkling of an eye. Three dogs descended upon them out of the night. Geraldine had avoided them on more than one occasion. However, she had been aware of their presence before they could detect her.

Geraldine and Romeo raced through the deserted streets, searching for high ground. The three dogs followed close behind, silent, ready for the kill. She and Romeo understood the peril, but felt no panic. It was as if the two of them dashed through the darkness in a protective bubble, in a nightmare they knew was not real. They jumped onto the narrow ledge of a fence high enough to provide them with a safe moment to catch their breath. The dogs broke their silence, barking and growling, jumping at the fence, frustrated at their inability to reach their prey. Geraldine and Romeo worked together, shape shifting into nightmarish creatures, eyes glowing, teeth bared, arching, bristling, challenging the dogs with dark, fiendish cries.

Romeo looked into Geraldine's eyes. His thoughts were calm and clear. "Go, my love. I will remain to distract them."

"No! I will not leave you."

"You must! The small ones need you."

The thought of her kittens tore at her heart. She knew that Romeo was right. She must escape and trust in the superiority of his feline intelligence to save him.

Suddenly one of the dogs managed to push through a loose board so they were able to jump at Geraldine and Romeo from both sides of the fence, cutting off the nearest avenue of escape.

Romeo searched the night for the best alternative. He indicated the roof of the house in the next yard. Geraldine considered inching her way along the narrow ledge to the back fence from which she could jump to safety. One misstep and she would fall into the grasp of their attackers. Their incessant barking wore on her nerves, making it difficult for her to concentrate.

"Jump, my love!" Romeo's thought reached her through the pandemonium.

The roof was the most logical escape route. She watched Romeo make his way carefully along the ledge, stopping occasionally to hiss and spit savagely at the dogs to keep their attention focused on him.

Geraldine hesitated, waiting for guidance. She knew she must risk it. If she remained safe, her kittens would be safe. She gauged the distance to the roof. A successful jump seemed impossible. She studied the distance again. The level of the roof was much higher than the ledge and it was slanted. She would have to leap from a sitting position without the advantage of momentum. There was little room on the ledge to maneuver her body into an ideal position for the jump. The memory of the pain in her right shoulder weakened her courage. She sat on her haunches with one paw at her chest, making several small preparatory movements, completing the jump in her mind.

In the midst of the noise and chaos, Geraldine remembered: "Faith will save a feline in the face of the impossible." She thanked the Highest One for creating her feline, leaned back slightly, and sailed through the night, digging her sharp claws into the shingles to support her landing.

Geraldine rushed across the roof, peering over each side,

searching desperately for some way to reach ground level. A trellis covered with clematis provided the only hope for escape. Her heart beat wildly as she dangled precariously from the edge of the roof, stretching the full length of her body to touch the trellis with her back paws. She dropped into the clematis, clawing frantically, slipping, sliding, clutching at the vine to break her fall. She tumbled to the ground and ran toward home with a speed she did not realize she possessed. She could still hear the barking dogs, so she was not certain Romeo had escaped. The life-threatening growls and barks gradually faded, and then disappeared.

Geraldine struggled to keep her focus. The night was still full of danger. Her heart and her mind split. She was desperate to get back to her kittens and equally desperate to know that Romeo was safe. He possessed courage, intelligence, and cunning, but the dogs were large, and there were three of them. She lost faith and slipped into fear—fear for Romeo, fear for herself, and fear for her kittens. The dogs had managed to surprise her. She had been careless tonight. She was terrified she had unwittingly endangered her family as well.

Geraldine was exhausted, but she would not rest. She could not seem to stop running. She was unable to dispel gruesome visions of howling, snarling creatures assaulting Romeo or predators like the Brotherhood savagely attacking Whisper, Beetle, and Tiptoe. She paused briefly, desperate to catch her breath, but a barking dog shattered the moment, and she bolted into the street.

Bright light momentarily blinded her. She hesitated just an instant and felt a blow to her body. She rolled over and over again to the other side of the street, landing on her feet and continuing at a full run. The car had grazed her, but she felt no pain, just the instinctive urge to reach her kittens. She did not stop running until she lay outside her den, panting, too exhausted to go any further, yet certain that her kittens were safe. When her breath returned to normal, she patiently examined her body for any sign of injury.

Geraldine had survived her ordeal. She thanked the Highest One repeatedly for sparing her and her kittens. She could not calm herself sufficiently to picture Romeo's thoughts and was tormented by the possibility that he did not survive. However, her priority now was her family.

Geraldine entered the den silently and lay down beside her kittens. Tiptoe and Whisper slept soundly. Beetle was dreaming. His body twitched. He whimpered and made running movements with his front legs. Geraldine hoped that his dreamtime was filled with happiness, not fear. She comforted herself with the thought that he might be reliving the delightful play he shared with Lightfoot. His squirming disturbed Tiptoe and Whisper. They merely rearranged themselves into more comfortable positions without really waking. She remembered her promise, but did not disturb them, grateful to rest at last.

Tiptoe raised her head. "Mother! You have been gone so long we all fell asleep. Whisper, Beetle, wake up! Mother is back."

"Did you see Fat Face?" Beetle asked immediately.

"Who cares," Whisper interrupted. "What about Father? Was he there?"

"Did you meet a Tree Climber?" asked Tiptoe, without waiting for her mother's answer.

Their curiosity seemed endless. Geraldine did her best to satisfy them, despite her fatigue. She recounted every detail of her experience until she came to the episode with the dogs. She did not want to frighten them unnecessarily. She finally decided they must know in order to fully comprehend the dangers of the night. She did not tell them she was uncertain about Romeo's fate.

"Now do you understand why I insisted that we would all be safer if I traveled to the Circle alone?"

The kittens each acknowledged the wisdom of their mother's decision.

"Shall we sleep?" Geraldine asked hopefully.

"And thank the Great Mother for guiding you home safely," added Tiptoe.

"The Tree Climber used a different name, little one. She called the source of all that exists, 'the Highest One.'"

"Then I shall use that name also!" Tiptoe gazed at her mother thoughtfully. "Do you think it matters what name we use?"

"I don't believe so. I feel the Tree Climber was simply trying to stretch our understanding beyond male and female . . . beyond feline . . ."

"I understand . . . to something beyond . . . everything."

"Why yes, my love."

"Well, I don't understand!" Beetle exclaimed without apology, anxious to reject what he could not comprehend. "Does it matter? Of course it doesn't matter! Great Mother . . . Highest One . . . Tree Climbers . . . what does any of this have to do with real life?"

"In time, many things will become clear. However, my loves, you must accept that you may never understand it all."

The kittens settled into their preferred positions around their mother, drawing close to her, more appreciative than ever of the security they felt in her presence.

Tiptoe gazed up at her mother with her large, soulful eyes. "Father is safe now."

Geraldine did not question her further. She only hoped that Tiptoe was right.

Geraldine lay beside her kittens, staring reverently at the delicate halos of light surrounding their bodies and the innocent beauty of their small faces. As she drifted somewhere between wakefulness and sleep, she received a clear, mental picture of Romeo enveloped in warmth and softness, asleep with his face buried in the fur of a large white canine, his back pressed into the curve of his human's body. Geraldine was finally able to release the world around her and escape into the forgetfulness of deep, profound sleep.

The High Ground

Chapter 26

Geraldine woke later than usual. She lay with her eyes half closed, purring contentedly, savoring the fragrance of the soft leaves beneath her, gently reentering the world. She sprang to her feet and rushed to the entrance of the den, suddenly aware that her kittens were not with her.

Tiptoe greeted her cheerfully. "Hello, Mother. We decided it was best to let you sleep."

"Is that so, little one!"

The kittens charged Geraldine playfully. She pretended to chase each of them, occasionally giving them the advantage, always teaching as well as playing. She experienced the full impact of her ordeal the previous night, discovering a new ache or pain every time she moved. She was so happy, the aches and pains seemed unimportant. She had weathered discomfort in the past and was grateful she had escaped serious injury. The kittens soon exhausted her and she stretched out on the leaves to rest.

"Well, my loves, I'm hungry. Shall we eat?"

Tiptoe, Beetle, and Whisper exchanged troubled looks, trying to decide who should respond to their mother's question.

Beetle stepped forward. "There's no food, Mother."

Geraldine worried their fate was about to change again. "No food?"
Tiptoe groaned. "Not anymore."

"There is a story here! Which one of you is going to tell me what happened? Beetle? Whisper? Tiptoe?"

Whisper answered. "Well . . . you were sleeping. We didn't want to disturb you."

"Yes."

"We watched the human put food out for us. We waited . . . a while."

Beetle interrupted. "You didn't wake up. We were hungry."

"We went down the hill," continued Whisper, "and before we realized it, we had eaten all of the food."

Tiptoe looked at her mother, full of apology. "You always eat first, but you never leave us without food. We are so sorry."

"Come close to me, little ones."

The kittens approached her wistfully. Whisper and Tiptoe were filled with remorse. Beetle seemed less penitent. Geraldine made deep eye contact with each of her kittens, especially Beetle. She felt his heart soften. "We are a family, my loves. We must take care of one another. Next time," Geraldine sighed, "wake me."

When Geraldine and her kittens returned to the patio for their evening meal, she ate sparingly. She realized that their appetites had outgrown the portions of food the human provided. They were not quite mature enough or skilled enough to hunt on their own, and it was unsafe for them to hunt with her too frequently.

The time for separation was drawing near. There was still so much Geraldine wanted to teach them before they began new lives without her. She was relieved that only a few experiences remained that she considered essential to their survival.

Chapter 27

Geraldine was amazed at how easily she slipped into her normal routine. The outward circumstances of her life did not change. She was once again preoccupied with the care and instruction of her kittens. She still had respiratory problems. Her symptoms were no longer periodic, just more or less severe. Her appetite had not improved. She had difficulty digesting what she did eat and she continued to lose weight. Despite her physical problems, a joyous energy pervaded her entire being.

Geraldine recognized that something deep inside her was changing, profoundly affecting her perception of the world around her. Her innate gratitude for the beauties in her life heightened. All of her senses sharpened. Colors seemed brighter, the fragrance of flowers more engaging, the touch of the sun more comforting. Everyday problems were less wearisome.

Her memories of Romeo were pleasant, not haunting. Sometimes she imagined that she sensed his presence in the night and felt comforted by it. Although she still held the desire to return to the Circle close to her heart, she was content at the end of each day to curl up with her kittens and postpone her visit to the next night. Days became weeks. Time passed quickly. Life flowed gently for her now.

Geraldine encountered the woman occasionally. The woman kept her distance, speaking to Geraldine softly, encouraging her to come closer. Geraldine longed to surrender, but would not yield until her kittens were fully trained to survive on their own. The woman continued to provide food and milk, and suddenly, one morning, the portions increased.

Each day the kittens grew more alert, healthy, and strong. Whisper and Beetle ran, jumped, and wrestled continuously unless they were eating or sleeping. Tiptoe was shedding some of her fear. She enjoyed enticing her brothers to chase her. She sometimes had difficulty managing her unusually long legs, but she could outrun both Whisper and Beetle. Lightfoot had taught her that speed could be her ally. She challenged her brothers, waited for their response until the last possible moment, her head and chest over her front legs, her hindquarters high in the air, and dashed toward her mother for protection, just in case. They played so energetically that Geraldine could no longer keep up with them. She usually stretched out under the tree on the patio, observing them with great pride.

Geraldine endured Beetle's endless questions about Fat Face. She assured herself that no kitten under her tutelage could possibly choose life as a Street Dweller. She was convinced that once Beetle actually experienced his father's beauty, he would choose his way of life over the dark ways of the Brotherhood.

Whisper and Tiptoe never tired of stories about Romeo and his bravery the night he helped Geraldine escape their canine attackers.

She had no idea how or when the meeting between her kittens and their father would take place. She was willing to allow the future to simply unfold.

Tiptoe never stopped asking when she would meet the Tree Climber. She continued to search the night sky for the Highest One. Geraldine watched Tiptoe's inner life flower and support her growth in the outer world. She continued to develop differently from her brothers. Although she appeared frail, she never lacked physical strength when she needed it. Geraldine did not understand this process. She simply observed it. Backstretch had promised to visit them when the time was right. She trusted that promise.

One morning she dozed on the patio, keeping at least one watchful eye on her kittens while they played. Tiptoe stretched out beside her to rest for a moment.

"Mother, I saw the Highest One."

Geraldine listened with a mixture of calm respect and wide-eyed curiosity.

"You saw what, little one?"

"Not in the way I see you now. I searched the darkness as I usually do, but I found nothing there. I saw on the inside . . . sort of like when we communicate without sound. I saw from the inside."

Geraldine pulled closer to her kitten. Tiptoe buried her muzzle in her mother's thick fur, and the two of them rested peacefully together.

Chapter 28

The kittens continued to spend their days exploring the hilltop or playing on the patio. Their lives revolved around the world of trees, grass, and flowers. Geraldine knew the time had come to acquaint them with the other world—the one humans had created. She had discovered a spot where they could observe the activities on a busy street and remain hidden. The kittens were elated when she informed them they were all going for a walk together. "Follow me closely," she cautioned.

Geraldine led her kittens to the outermost rim of the hilltop where she had discovered a broken slat in the fence. She had used it to pass into the next yard whenever her kittens were unable to observe her. They were doing more and more exploring without her, and she knew they would soon chance upon it on their own.

Geraldine stepped through the opening in the fence and signaled her kittens to follow. Their bodies tensed and their eyes widened with excitement as they stepped beyond the boundaries of the world they knew. She sensed their high spirits and watched them closely. She was particularly concerned about Beetle. The moment he moved out of line she gave him a solid cuff with her paw and a sharp cry. Her lack of patience puzzled her as much as it did her kittens.

"We're not stopping here!" she growled.

"Why?"

Geraldine calmed herself. "What I want to show you is far more exciting."

"What? What, Mother? Yes, what?" They all asked simultaneously.

"It is something that you must see for yourself. We will be there soon."

Beetle wanted to explore this new territory now. Whisper pressed his head against his brother's long, slender neck. "Let's go! We can come back here anytime."

Beetle decided Whisper was right. Besides, his mother's paw was poised for another slap.

Geraldine had never encountered humans or their pets in the next two yards in the early morning, but she would not cross them in the open. They were both fringed with shrubs and small trees, so she guided her kittens along the perimeters using the plants as cover. She had previously located at least one place along each fence where it was possible to pass into the next yard with a minimum amount of digging and had prepared the way for herself and her kittens. They made it successfully through the two adjoining yards and finally approached their last obstacle, a wire fence lightly intertwined with ivy.

Geraldine stood straight and motionless. The kittens immediately mimicked her. She listened to the dull thud of digging and the clang of garden tools. She knew from past experience an elderly human was working in his yard. Most humans followed a fairly predictable routine. This one was an exception. He had chased her away on more than one occasion with hostile sounds and gestures. She attributed his behavior to the territorial instinct shared by most creatures and responded to him the way she did to all humans—she avoided him.

The attention of Tiptoe and Whisper was fixed on the sounds beyond the fence. Beetle observed his mother intensely, absorbing her feelings about the human.

Whisper tilted his head slowly from side to side. "What are those sounds, Mother?"

Geraldine searched for an explanation. "It is impossible for me to explain. You must see for yourself in order to understand."

The kittens pressed close to the fence and peered through the ivy.

"Oh," observed Whisper in a detached, objective manner, "a human. What is he doing?"

Beetle eyed him suspiciously. "I don't like him! He doesn't like felines."

"Why are you so certain?" asked Tiptoe.

"I just know!"

Whisper's interest sharpened. "The human doesn't like green creatures. He is destroying them."

Tiptoe was not convinced. "Maybe he is going to eat them. Is that it, Mother? Do humans eat green creatures like we do?"

"Yes, but I have watched the human do this in the past. He will probably destroy them, not eat them."

Tiptoe found this puzzling. "Why?"

"Sometimes humans deliberately nourish green creatures, and sometimes they deliberately destroy them."

"Why?" insisted Whisper.

"I spent the first part of my life with humans. My mother spent her entire life with them. Despite her teaching and my experience, there are still many things about them I do not understand."

The kittens were fascinated. They observed everything about the human, particularly his hands and the tools he used.

"Our bodies are sufficient to accomplish all of our tasks," Geraldine explained. "The body of the human is not." She indicated the garden tools. "They make use of those as well."

"Didn't I tell you?" Beetle looked back at his mother. "Everything about humans is complicated!"

"There is a reason, little one. They seem determined to change everything around them to satisfy their desires. They solve many problems, but they invariably create others. This keeps them very busy."

Geraldine surveyed their surroundings. "It is cool and pleasant here. We may as well rest for a while." She gave Beetle a sharp glance. "We must be very quiet. Hopefully, the human will leave soon."

Geraldine sniffed the pleasing scent of damp soil and found the ideal spot on which to recline, still watching for any sign of mischief. The kittens continued to observe the human, their ears alert, and their eyes unblinking.

The sun moved across the sky. Flecks of sunshine fell here and there through the shrubbery. The sounds beyond the fence continued.

Beetle became restless. "You told us he would be leaving soon."

"He will, my love. Be patient."

Beetle was sick to death of patience. He reached the limit of his endurance when the sounds finally stopped. Geraldine moved silently toward the fence. She listened to the elderly gentleman pick up his tools, walk to his house, and shut the back door.

"There it is, my loves, the final sound." Geraldine was as relieved as her kittens. "Remember, we must still be cautious. Follow me." She slowly crawled under the fence with her kittens close behind. Once again they skirted the edge of the yard until they reached a wire fence on the opposite side of the garden thickly overgrown with ivy. Geraldine guided her kittens to a spot where the vines were less dense, permitting them to observe a main thoroughfare on the other side. It was a broad street, lined with houses and a few small shops.

"The space is limited. Be considerate of one another and share it."

Beetle squeezed Whisper and Tiptoe to the back.

"We can't see!" Whisper complained.

"Move over, Beetle!" Geraldine commanded. "You must each be able to observe. This is why we are here."

It was mid-morning. Several people walked briskly along the sidewalk. A man and a woman sat down on a bench near a bus stop. The rest continued on their way. Cars occasionally zipped by from both directions. Whisper and Tiptoe turned toward their mother slowly, their faces full of questions. Beetle was no longer aware of his mother or his littermates. He immersed himself in the strange scene unfolding before him. Geraldine mewed urgently, but softly, to get his attention.

"Observe everything carefully, my loves. One day you may want to cross from one side to the other side and . . ."

"No, Mother!" Tiptoe interrupted. "Not ever! I will stay as far away from this place as I can. I don't like it here. It's too noisy."

Whisper agreed. "It smells bad, too!"

Beetle continued to stare through the fence, absorbing every detail of the activity on the street.

Geraldine thought for a moment. "One day circumstances may force you to cross to the other side."

"Oh," sighed Tiptoe, "I hope not."

Whisper shared his sister's misgivings. "I can't imagine anything that would make me want to do that."

Geraldine nuzzled her kittens to reassure them. "It is frightening at first because there is no way to practice this skill. Trust your instincts and believe that, in time, it will become routine to you."

The kittens looked through the fence at the steady flow of traffic. Whisper and Tiptoe found it difficult to believe that crossing a busy street would ever become routine. Beetle's eyes glistened with excitement. He was eager to test his powers.

"Remember, my loves, the moving objects can approach you from both directions. Timing is essential. Patience is crucial. Trust the Knowing, focus straight ahead, gallop to the other side without hesitation."

Whisper and Tiptoe stared at each other, determined to avoid the situation at all costs. Beetle was certain he could master this skill. Geraldine watched him closely.

"Never underestimate the danger. If one of the objects touches you, your body may sleep forever. Do you understand?"

Tiptoe and Whisper exchanged somber looks. "Yes, Mother."

Beetle's eyes darkened. He was not afraid of life. He was afraid of death.

Geraldine mewed gently. "Be cautious. Trust your feline instincts. They are formidable. Watch a while longer. Remember what you see. We must leave soon to return to the den safely."

The kittens absorbed themselves in the street activity. Geraldine prepared to relax. She was particularly fond of this garden. The ground was soft and pliable. It was an exhilarating experience to dig here and to recline because the earth shaped itself so easily to the contours of her body. She lay back, purring softly.

Tiptoe turned her lovely head toward her mother. "I see, Mother, that in many ways, humans are just like us."

Beetle grimaced at the thought.

Tiptoe continued. "There are males and females, mothers and little ones. They are different shapes and sizes. However, their coats are far more colorful than ours. Look at that one!" Tiptoe indicated a woman with a child toddling beside her, dressed in primary colors.

"Oh, no, little one! Humans are different colors, but they do not have coats like ours to protect them. They put on the colors you are observing when they need warmth and protection. They remove them when they do not."

"Oh my," thought Tiptoe sympathetically.

"Humans make everything complicated," grumbled Beetle.

The kittens stopped sharing thoughts. All three of them sat up straight and still, their bodies tense and their ears forward. They had felt the vibrations before they could see or hear the source. Geraldine lay quietly, observing their responses.

Whisper and Tiptoe glanced at their mother nervously, puzzled by her calm, and looked back through the fence. They hesitated a moment longer, caught between fear and curiosity, and then dove behind her body for protection. Beetle steadied himself. He watched the huge, threatening object grow even larger as it moved toward him. A bus roared to a stop directly in front of their hiding place, and he decided to join his littermates.

Tiptoe pressed closer to her mother. "What kind of creature is that?"

Beetle could no longer repress his curiosity and, before Geraldine could respond, he peeked around her body, stretching his neck as far as he could without relinquishing her protection.

Tiptoe and Whisper watched him tensely. "What do you see?" asked Whisper. "What is it?"

Beetle sat back on his haunches, relieved and a little disappointed. "It's not a creature at all. It's just like the other moving things, only bigger."

Tiptoe sat up just as the bus finished taking on passengers. "And look! Look, Whisper!" She nudged her brother gently. "There are humans inside!"

Whisper found the odor surrounding the bus so repulsive he kept his nose buried in his mother's fur. Geraldine licked his head affectionately.

Tiptoe nudged her brother again. "There are humans inside all of the moving things. But, why, Mother?"

"They use them to get from one place to another."

"But, why?"

"Perhaps because they can get where they want to go faster."

Tiptoe still did not understand. "But, why?"

"They keep themselves very busy and are constantly rushing from here to there."

"Are they content to be so busy?"

"I'm not certain, my love."

Tiptoe found this information fascinating. "Whisper!" She scolded her brother. "You're not watching!"

Whisper lifted his head slowly, cautiously sniffing the air just as the bus pulled away from the curb and surged forward down the street. The odor overwhelmed him once again. "Mother, how do humans stand the smell and the noise?"

"When I lived with my human family I noticed that their sense of smell was poor and that they didn't hear all of the sounds that I did. They don't always see well either."

"Really?"

"And they are helpless in the dark."

"Poor things!" thought Tiptoe, with genuine compassion.

"But as I told you, they are clever. They find ways to compensate for these limitations."

Whisper had crept forward to stare through the fence at something that puzzled him. "Mother, where are all the green creatures?"

"Humans are builders, my love. Many creatures are like that."

Whisper thought hard. "Yes, the crawlers build."

"And the flyers. You will encounter others as your experience grows. But humans build enormous dens. Sometimes they destroy green creatures to make room for them."

"Why are their dens always so big?"

"Humans use them for many purposes, not just for rest and protection. They spend most of their time in them, or traveling from one den to another."

"Why?"

"They are large creatures, but quite vulnerable. Perhaps they feel safer inside."

Tiptoe was intrigued. "What is it like inside their dens?"

"Very pleasant, little one. Humans are as fond of warmth and comfort as we are. There are many soft places for sleep and relaxation."

"What else?" asked Whisper.

"It is too difficult for me to explain. One day you will see for yourself."

"Never!" growled Beetle. "I don't understand. Humans don't hear as well as we do. They don't see as well as we do. Our sense of smell is better. They are so weak and helpless they have to cover themselves with color for protection. They build huge dens and hide in them to feel safe. Why do they think they're so special?"

"Beetle!" Tiptoe was perturbed by her brother's lack of compassion. "Humans are not as self-sufficient as we are. They need us. We can help them."

"Never!"

"You many change your mind one day."

"Never!"

Whisper considered their thoughts while he carefully studied each person who walked by. "Mother, I have observed the light around the body of each human who passes. The light is usually narrow and cloudy rather than broad and bright. Why?"

"Many humans live in fear. They are as afraid of each other as they are of other creatures."

"I understand! That's why they use so much energy just to protect themselves."

"Yes, my love, fear is a habit with them."

Geraldine and her family returned safely to the hilltop. The kittens immediately began to play. Geraldine lay panting until she could breathe normally again. Her eyes ran with fluid, her nasal passages were congested, and she sneezed several times in rapid succession. She was surprised at the depth of her fatigue. She stretched out in front of the den, resting until her kittens tired of their games and joined her.

Geraldine was grateful for this day of adventure and discovery with her family. She was equally grateful when her kittens finally curled up next to her and fell asleep.

Chapter 29

Geraldine's symptoms continued to ease and then grow worse. Sometimes her breathing was so labored she found it difficult to sleep through the night. One morning she left the den quite early, emerging into the quiet beauty of predawn, revitalized by the brisk, clean air. The moon was still high in the sky, the orange glow of the sun hovered just beneath the horizon. She remained near the den until potentially threatening creatures like the raccoon had retired for the day. After a routine search for evidence of intruders, she seized the opportunity to delight her discriminating taste buds and quench her persistent thirst at the water barrel.

Geraldine wandered from yard to yard over familiar paths, alert for any significant changes. She eventually approached her favorite spot. It was much too early to encounter the elderly human, so she slipped under the fence, anticipating the satisfaction she would experience scratching a soft place in the loose soil and stretching out for a short nap. She barely emerged from the shrubbery when she scented a raccoon. She quickly recognized it had been trapped. Tosey had shown her a lure of this kind and warned her of its dangers. She kept her distance and closely observed the animal as it paced back and forth in confusion, desperate to escape its prison.

The raccoon immediately sensed Geraldine's presence and pressed its body against the back of the cage, hissing and growling. She had never been this close to a predator without peril. Her curiosity was so intense she abandoned the protection of the shrubs, slowly moving forward to observe it further. The frenzied creature lunged at her; she recoiled instinctively, reassured herself, and moved forward again. She circled the cage, drawing closer, her mouth slightly open, her sensitive nostrils flared, recording every scent that provided information.

Geraldine saw that food had been left as the lure, just as she expected. She found it alarming that its scent matched the food the woman put out for her each day. In an intuitive flash she knew the trap had been intended for her, not the raccoon. The elderly human had definitely objected to her presence. She wondered if the woman also wanted to be rid of her. However, she experienced no premonition of danger or instinctive urge to move her kittens.

Geraldine was now right next to the cage, mesmerized by the close proximity of a natural enemy who could do her no harm. She felt genuine compassion for the imprisoned creature and gratitude that she had escaped its fate. She was about to attempt communication when the sound of the human entering the backyard broke the spell. She withdrew into the shrubs, pulled herself under the fence into the next yard, and sprinted toward the hilltop.

Geraldine slowed to a walk to catch her breath, scanning the area for a safe place to pause. She passed a large tree with a huge trunk that expanded into a maze of thick branches, crisscrossing one another toward the sky. The Tree Climber entered her thoughts. She considered the intriguing possibility of a safe haven somewhere in the high, massive branches.

Geraldine felt incredibly at ease climbing the tree, despite her fatigue. There was no need to rush. She had plenty of time before her kittens would become impatient to leave the safety of the den. The tree limbs were broad and sturdy even at great height. Her feline instincts prodded her upward in search of the perfect spot, rewarding her effort with the discovery of an ideal place for a nap.

A gang of boisterous crows occupying the uppermost branches swarmed around the tree, protesting her arrival. They eventually accepted her presence and returned to their perches. Geraldine trimmed and sharpened her claws on the bark and decided she liked the feeling of her newly discovered retreat. As she yawned, stretched, and reclined in a cozy hollow, she received a confusing mental picture of Tiptoe. She was unable to make sense of it. There was no feeling of danger, so she curled up and dozed lightly.

Geraldine woke just in time to watch the sun slowly break above the horizon. She had never witnessed the glowing orb emerge from its hiding place to begin its ascent. She decided to return the next morning to see if this magnificent event repeated itself in the same way each day.

Geraldine gazed at a broad vista from a high perspective. This new vantage point provided an arresting view of her everyday world. She was amazed at how much she could see, and how little she could see. Large objects appeared small. Small objects became tiny or invisible. "What seems to be is not always what is," she thought, mesmerized by the reality unfolding before her. She also realized she was looking down on her old world with none of the dire consequences her mother had predicted.

Geraldine was lost in wonder, expanding her experience beyond most ground dwellers, glimpsing life from the point of view of flying creatures. Flocks of birds in precise formation flapped and soared past her field of vision. Others came to rest in the treetop. She had no desire to disturb them, and they seemed to understand. The appearance of a magnificent blue heron tested her belief in her own eyes. She stared in astonishment at its huge wingspan and the length of its neck and tapered bill. She could hardly wait to tell her kittens and her friends in the Circle that such a creature existed.

Breathless wonder replaced Geraldine's innate appreciation of the immensity and diversity of the world around her. She discovered awesome beauty, peace, and refuge in the treetop.

Chapter 30

The morning sky brightened as Geraldine trotted back to her den. She approached the upper patio cautiously. The food was in the usual place. She took a few bites, drank an immense amount of water, and turned to climb the hill. She had only taken a few steps when she looked back toward the patio, startled by the sound of the woman's voice. She was standing on the top step, calling to her gently. Geraldine could not understand how she failed to anticipate her appearance.

Neither of them moved. Eventually, the woman broke the tension, leaning forward to extend her hand. Geraldine considered a quick retreat. However, she was as curious as she was wary. She walked slowly toward the woman, pausing several times to observe her response. She perceived no threat. The woman did not change her position and continued to speak softly. Geraldine was now close enough to thoroughly sniff the extended hand. In spite of herself, she rubbed her head against it and began to purr. She withdrew abruptly when the woman reached out to touch her.

Her patroness soothed her with quiet, caressing tones. Once again, Geraldine took slow, halting steps forward until she was close enough to allow the woman to stroke her head and scratch her softly behind her ears. For a moment, Geraldine was held captive by her feelings, by a deep desire for relationship with the human. When the woman reached down to pick her up, she yielded to her inner guidance and retreated a safe distance.

Geraldine turned to scurry up the hill and was shocked to see three small heads peeking above the grass, watching the drama unfold. Her fear for her kittens' safety exploded in hot, sudden anger. She charged up the hillside and chased them back to the den in a fit of temper. She stopped outside the den to regain her composure, filled with regret for her overreaction, trying to understand why her level of irritation had steadily increased over the past weeks. "Perhaps it is time to end my isolation and visit old friends," she thought.

As Geraldine entered the den, the sight of her three kittens huddled together, dreading what might happen next, pinched her heart. They had never experienced this level of anger from her. "My loves, I owe you an apology for my outburst . . . I . . ." She stopped mid-thought to gather all of her feline wits about her. The mental picture of Tiptoe she had found so confusing suddenly became clear.

"Tiptoe?"

"Yes, Mother."

"Again?"

"I tried to stop her!" Beetle squeezed in before Tiptoe could respond. He added indignantly, "She ignored me!"

Geraldine smiled inside. "Come, my loves." She reclined, inviting the kittens to lie down next to her. "I am sorry. It is better to keep your temper than to lose it. It is only important for you to know that you are angry."

Tiptoe snuggled closer to her mother. "We lose our temper when we are afraid."

"Yes, Tiptoe, I lost my temper because I was afraid."

Tiptoe's lustrous green eyes filled with empathy and warm understanding. "You were afraid for us, Mother. There is no reason to fear this human. Please believe me."

"I agree, my love. There is no present danger. I did stumble across something earlier that I must discuss with you. Do you remember the human we encountered on our last outing?"

"Him? Of course we do!" answered Beetle, annoyed by the memory.

"We must avoid his territory. There is danger there."

Beetle burned with curiosity. "What kind of danger?"

"I will explain later. But first Tiptoe, tell me what happened."

"I heard the human leave her den much earlier than usual. I listened carefully to the sounds she was making and determined that she was not putting food out for us. It was much too early for that anyway. Naturally we were all curious about what she was doing. Isn't that true?" She looked to her brothers for support.

Beetle was antagonistic as usual. "I can care less what the human is up to."

Tiptoe gave Beetle an irritated look and continued.

"Anyway, all three of us crawled to the edge of the hill."

"Really?" asked Geraldine. "You too, Beetle?"

"Well, yes."

"Oh. Were you able to see much from way up here?"

"No, Mother. That was the problem. We had to climb down . . . cautiously of course . . . to our eating-place to see anything at all."

"I understand. Then what?"

"We saw her sitting, all covered in color . . . I think . . . drinking something. That's all she did . . . for the longest time. Then she rose and returned to her den."

"Then what?"

"We did not hear the final sound. We heard jumbled sounds . . . unfamiliar . . . mysterious sounds."

"Naturally you were curious."

"Oh yes, Mother. I decided I must investigate further."

"That's when we parted company. I told her those sounds were not worth investigating. I told her we should return to the den," complained Beetle, his practical nature offended by what he considered foolish behavior.

"You left?"

"Was I supposed to put myself in danger because of her bad judgment? I told her she was just going to get us all in trouble."

"You went back to the den?"

"Not exactly. I remained at the edge of the hill and kept watch."

"Oh. What about you Whisper?"

"She was determined to go. I could do nothing to stop her. I remained where I was in case she needed my help."

"So, Tiptoe, what did you do next?"

"I reached our eating-place and then had to climb downward again . . . a long way. It was far more difficult than I expected. I almost tumbled over myself a couple of times. When I finally reached the bottom I hid among the green creatures and listened. The sounds were clearer, but I needed to get closer."

"Oh my. Then what?"

"I was faced with a steep climb upward . . . so steep I had to pull myself up to each level. It was hard, Mother, but I kept going," Tiptoe announced proudly. "When I finally reached the top, she was there, surrounded by pleasant, soothing, beautiful sounds and," she gave Whisper a provocative look, "appetizing scents. We were separated by something, but I could see her through it."

"Ah! I understand!"

"I never stopped looking up, Mother. It was quite an experience. Humans, as well as everything they keep around them, are so big!"

"Yes, my love."

"She did not notice me immediately. I just listened to the sounds and watched her moving about, doing things here and doing things there. But then, I couldn't resist. I called to her."

"You made your presence known?"

"Yes, *finally!*"

"Did she invite you into her den?"

"We observed each other for some time. When she removed the separation, I decided to leave. I was not prepared to go any further— not until I consulted you first. I was just curious."

"Did she pursue you?"

"No."

Geraldine was uncertain how to interpret the woman's behavior.

"I climbed downward . . . more easily this time. However, when I began the climb upward, I was tired and experienced some difficulty. The human was suddenly behind me. I felt her approach. There was nothing I could do . . . it happened so quickly. She picked me up, carried me to our eating-place, released me gently, and left. I immediately hid among the green creatures until I heard the final sound."

"Did she see you, Whisper?"

"No."

"You, Beetle?"

"No."

"Well, it doesn't matter. She may now be aware that there are three of you."

Tiptoe searched her mother's eyes for understanding. "Something else happened."

"What, my love?"

"It has happened before."

"Tell us, my love."

"As I waited among the green creatures, a group of them, glowing with color, living separate from the others, called to me sweetly. 'Ground Dweller! We trust the human. She cares for us faithfully.'"

"You expect me to believe that?" Beetle cried.

"Just because you don't communicate with green creatures doesn't mean I can't!"

"Brother," Whisper stated quietly, "it is true."

"What? You too?"

"Beetle, my love." Geraldine tried to soothe him. "Such things are possible."

"Not green creatures!"

"Yes, Beetle. Green creatures."

Tiptoe appealed to her mother. "I trust the human. I want to be her Companion."

"The time has come to discuss the possibility."

"Then, I am old enough now?"

"Yes, but your training is incomplete. If she accepts you, and circumstances change—as they did for me—you must be able to survive on your own."

"Oh, they won't change. I am certain of that."

"There is something else to consider. I must continue to train your brothers. If you join her, you must leave us . . . indefinitely. It may be better for your brothers and me if the human thinks we have gone."

Tiptoe's glittering eyes darkened for a moment and then filled again with light. "Maybe she will accept all of us!"

"Not me!" Beetle made his intention clear. "I'd rather be a Street Dweller any day."

"Don't be concerned," Geraldine assured him. "I don't believe the human would ever accept our entire family."

"Then I cannot leave now," Tiptoe announced without a trace of sadness. "I will wait until the time is right for all of us."

"I feel this is best for you as well as for us. We are safe for now."

"Mother, the human will not harm us."

"I agree, my love. Not intentionally. We must still be cautious."

"I have an idea," suggested Whisper.

Beetle could never resist baiting his brother. He rolled toward him quickly, pawing at his face, biting his shoulder playfully. "I hope it's better than the last one."

Whisper instinctively rolled away to avoid him. "Which one was that?"

"I don't remember, but it wasn't any good."

"Oh, stop!" Tiptoe knew Beetle was just goading his brother. "He is playing with you again. What is your idea?"

"My idea?" Whisper was still a little confused. "Oh . . . why don't we promise one another . . . right now . . . that we will remain together as a family until Mother is satisfied we are all fully trained."

Beetle was not certain he wanted to make such a promise. He was only willing to submit to his mother's authority long enough to master the necessary survival skills. "But I always learn faster than either of you."

Geraldine corrected him. "That is true about some things, but not about others."

Beetle reflected for some time, trusting his mother's love and her judgment, yet yearning for independence. He finally yielded. "I will wait. It can't take that much longer."

Whisper charged Beetle good-naturedly. "You actually considered your decision before you made it. There may be hope for you."

Beetle jumped forward aggressively to engage him. He was surprised when Whisper did not sidestep his attack. "There may be hope for you, too."

Geraldine was pleased. "Then we agree. We will not separate until the day you have all completed your training."

"Tiptoe?"

"I agree."

"Whisper?"

"I agree."

"Beetle?"

"Yes . . . I agree."

"That day is very close, little ones."

Tiptoe pulled herself closer to her mother. "We will miss you so much!"

Whisper wanted to reassure his sister. "It isn't as if we will never see one another again." Something in his mother's demeanor troubled him. "We will see one another again, won't we?"

"I don't know, Whisper. I have not seen my family since I was taken from them. You must prepare yourself for that possibility."

"You visit your friends in the Circle. Why can't we visit one another?"

"These are things we cannot know right now."

Whisper struggled to remain optimistic. "Maybe we could all meet again in the Circle."

"That is possible."

Geraldine remembered the day she left her mother. "Separation is never easy."

Tiptoe's brilliant eyes illuminated from deep within. "Even if we have to be apart physically, we will always be connected."

"Yes, my loves, always."

Chapter 31

Geraldine explained to the kittens why they must avoid the old gentleman's territory. She shared mental pictures with them about the appearance of a trap and warned that food was used as a lure. However, she decided to wait a while longer before telling them about her experience in the treetop.

Geraldine was aware that she was slowly losing both her desire to eat and to drink. She asked less of herself physically these days so her lack of strength was manageable. She delayed her visit to the Circle, hoping her condition would improve. She finally convinced herself that time spent with Romeo and her old friends would be the perfect remedy. She also waited until it was likely Romeo would attend. She longed to see him and wanted to pave the way for a meeting between her kittens and their father.

One warm, sunny afternoon, Geraldine experienced a surge of optimistic energy as she lay, serenely content, watching her kittens play. She promised herself she would sit in the Circle that night. Naturally, the kittens wanted to accompany her. Geraldine reminded them of the dangers inherent in any night journey. They were mature enough to understand that their presence might compromise her safety.

"It isn't time yet, is it?" Tiptoe conceded, dropping her chin to her chest, anticipating her mother's response.

"No, my love. Not yet."

"It will be soon!" Beetle announced confidently, his tall ears pricked upward.

"Yes, my love, soon."

Whisper looked at his mother with his striking gold eyes. "And, will we meet Father soon?"

"Yes, my love, soon."

"But is it safe for you to go?" Tiptoe was uncertain why she felt such concern.

"I promise I will be most cautious. Will each of you spare me a great deal of anxiety and promise to remain in the den until I return?"

"We agree," they responded almost in unison.

Geraldine left the hilltop in good spirits. She had only gone a short distance when her legs felt abnormally heavy. The fatigue spread quickly throughout her body. She realized she had lost some stamina, but did not anticipate she would tire this rapidly. She compensated for her lack of energy by traveling slowly and resting when necessary.

Geraldine continued on until she suddenly felt dizzy. Her environment spun wildly for a moment, leaving her disoriented. She struggled to control her body. She recognized that something was drastically wrong and tried to calm herself, waiting patiently in the shadows for these sensations to pass. She gradually regained her equilibrium, but decided to return home immediately.

The reprieve was temporary. Within minutes an odd numbness pervaded the lower half of her body. Her back legs wobbled and she staggered forward with great difficulty. She could no longer focus clearly, nor was she certain of her direction. Instinct guided her as her body progressively failed. She stumbled to the pavement overwhelmed by the feeling that she could not continue. Her love for her kittens strengthened her will and she pulled herself to her feet, persevering in her determined struggle to reach them.

Geraldine sensed she was approaching the woman's house when she lost control of her back legs. She crawled rather than give up, ripping the tender pads on her front paws as she dragged herself across the pavement. She reached the hedge bordering the driveway and collapsed, unable to will her body to move.

"No!" she cried into the night. "I must get home! I must return to my little ones!"

Geraldine hoped this moment would pass and her strength would return. She lay there for some time, motionless, trapped in a body that could not obey. All of her efforts to move were futile. She had never experienced such vulnerability. As she slipped in and out of consciousness, every sound she perceived tossed her into a state of terror until it eventually passed into the night. She lost heart and howled in anguish, but the sound was locked inside.

Geraldine thought she saw a spot of light in the distance. She strained to identify the source. Her feline senses could not penetrate the haze that enveloped her. She fought to quell her panic as the light flashed erratically and new sounds drew close. Once again the Tree

Climber entered her mind. "Faith will save a feline in the face of the impossible." She surrendered her fate to the Highest One and waited.

A hand reached down to touch her bearing a scent she recognized immediately. Was it possible the woman had heard her silent cry for help? Geraldine's spirits lifted, only to fall. A moment later there was only emptiness. She remembered nothing more.

Chapter 32

The woman recognized Geraldine as the stray cat she had been feeding. She rushed back to her house to get a towel, wrapped it gently around the animal's limp body, and placed the fragile bundle on the front seat of her car. As she backed out of the driveway to take the stray to the emergency clinic, she saw an unusually large cat observing her. She noticed it because of its size and its striking white coat with black markings. When she looked again, it had disappeared.

The woman placed the stray in the capable hands of a veterinarian. She could not bring herself to leave and insisted on remaining with the animal as long as possible.

Geraldine slowly regained consciousness lying on her side under a bright light. She felt strangely detached from her body. The feeling was pleasant until a mental picture of her three kittens pierced her dreamlike state. She could not identify her surroundings. She heard human voices she did not recognize. She felt the life force draining from her body. Panic swept through her entire being. She cursed her helplessness as she fought to hang onto life. "*I will not leave my little ones.*"

Once again, Geraldine sensed the woman's presence. She felt her moving closer and welcomed her scent and the sound of her reassuring whispers. The woman's presence calmed her terrified heart, replacing her anguish over Tiptoe, Whisper, and Beetle with a sense of hope and wonder. She stopped struggling and allowed herself to drift with the Knowing that her kittens would be safe. Loving images of her mother, the little human, and Romeo filled Geraldine's mind, purging any remnant of fear. At her last moment of consciousness, she nestled her head into Romeo's long, silky fur and slipped into peaceful oblivion.

The woman rested her elbows on the table and encircled the stray cat with her arms. Her eyes filled with tears at the sight of its thin, worn body and the torn, bloody pads on its front paws. It occurred to her that every creature on earth— man or beast—has a story. She wondered about the sorrows this small animal had endured and fervently wished its story a happy ending.

One huge tear escaped the woman's control, spilling down her cheek onto the still body in the circle of her arms. She straightened up and studied the stray thoroughly. She traced the scarab marking on its forehead slowly with her index finger and left the treatment room trapped in sadness.

The vet warned that Geraldine's chance for survival was slim. "It will take a miracle," he added. Since the animal did not appear to be suffering, the woman decided to wait until morning before making a final decision. He assured her that he was doing everything possible. She managed a half smile and thanked him.

"Do you believe in miracles?" she asked.

"I'm not sure. I have certainly witnessed recoveries science cannot explain."

"What do you think caused the unexplained recoveries?"

"My field is veterinary science, but I do have a personal opinion."

"Tell me."

"Love."

The woman shook her head quickly in agreement. "We all need to be loved."

"I suppose that's true. However, I suspect it is the capacity *to* love that creates miracles."

Chapter 33

The call of a solitary bird disturbed the quiet on the early morning hillside. Tiptoe sat up abruptly, trembling with a chilling dread.

"Beetle! Whisper! Wake up! Mother hasn't returned yet!"

"Don't worry." Whisper tried to reassure her. "I'm sure Mother is fine. She returned late the last time she visited the Circle."

Beetle was irritated with his sister for interrupting his sleep. "You worry about everything! Go back to sleep."

"But . . ." Tiptoe realized they were no longer listening. She tried to regain her calm, but could not dispel her anxiety. Tiptoe was certain something had happened to her mother.

The den suddenly filled with light. Tiptoe cowered. She cried out hopefully, "Mother, is that you?"

"There is nothing to fear, little one. Soon you and your brothers will leave the dark security of the den. Go to the bottom of the hill when it is light and wait there."

"But Mother . . . where are you?" She began to shiver uncontrollably. "It is so cold here without you."

"Release your fear, little one. Love will guide you."

The den was suddenly dark again.

"Beetle! Whisper! Please wake up. Something strange just happened . . . and Mother still isn't home!"

"What happened?" Whisper was deeply concerned. "Look, she's shivering."

"I saw something . . . maybe it was Mother . . . except she isn't here."

Whisper tried to comfort his sister. "Perhaps you were just dreaming."

"But Mother isn't home yet!"

"Will you relax?" Beetle gave his sister an impatient look. "Mother always comes home."

Tiptoe cuddled close to her brothers. Beetle and Whisper fell asleep easily. Tiptoe could not curb her restlessness. She finally stationed herself at the entrance of the den so that she could greet her mother the minute she appeared.

Darkness turned to light. Whisper and Beetle woke to discover there was still no sign of their mother. They joined Tiptoe at the opening to the den.

"Where can Mother be?" Tiptoe asked again and again.

Whisper had grown accustomed to regular meals. "And the human? She has not brought food!"

"You can't depend on humans for anything," Beetle reminded his brother. "We can depend on Mother. She will return."

It was full daylight when the kittens began to argue about what they should do next. Tiptoe decided she must tell them about the instructions she had received.

"What?" Beetle was angry. "Why should we expose ourselves to danger? There's no food down there anyway. Mother is probably on her way home right now. I say we wait here!"

Whisper was willing to compromise. "We can wait a while longer. If Mother does not return, and there is no sign of the human, let's go down to our eating-place. There are plenty of places to hide if danger comes."

"Go if you want to. I am staying here."

Beetle had made up his mind. Whisper and Tiptoe could only hope their mother would return and spare them this decision.

However, by mid-afternoon she had still not come home, and the human had not brought them food. The kittens were confused, grief stricken, and hungry.

Whisper sensed it was time to act. "Mother is able to communicate with us—even at a distance. The only communication we have received has been through Tiptoe . . ."

"And," interrupted Beetle, "who knows where that came from."

Whisper was forced to agree. He faced the first difficult decision of his young life. He did what he had been taught. He quieted himself for a moment and waited for guidance. "We must go now." Whisper was amazed by his own certainty. "We must go with Tiptoe."

"No!" Beetle insisted. "Mother will return. She wanted us to wait here."

Whisper begged his brother. "Please come with us."

"No!"

Whisper and Tiptoe agonized over leaving their brother behind. They walked slowly from the den, hoping he would change his mind. They had almost reached the edge of the hill when they heard the familiar sounds signaling the arrival of the human. Whisper felt his hope renew. "Hurry, Beetle! The human is coming!"

Whisper, Tiptoe, and Beetle hid in the high grass, expecting the woman to climb the stairs as usual. When she did not appear, they began to argue again.

In the midst of the chaos, Tiptoe recalled her previous experience with the human. She tried to get her brothers' attention. "Something important just occurred to me." She forced herself to jump between them. "Will you stop fighting long enough to listen?"

Whisper stepped back. "Tiptoe is right. This is getting us nowhere."

"The human has apparently returned to her den, yet we have not heard the final sound. Don't you wonder why? Let's climb down to our eating-place . . . just to get a better look."

"No!" Beetle would not yield.

Whisper was resolute. "I'm going with Tiptoe."

The two kittens slinked down the hill to the patio and peeked through the bushes. The woman was nowhere in sight.

"Listen, Whisper . . . the sounds! Listen!" They heard the music that had led Tiptoe to the woman's back door on the first occasion.

"Wait here."

"No, Tiptoe!" Whisper objected.

"You remain here as we were instructed. I must go."

Tiptoe did not wait for her brother's approval. She crawled down the stairs with increasing skill and hid. Intense curiosity had muted her fear the first time she approached the woman's house. Now the stairs seemed farther away and the climb to the porch impossibly steep. She heard the green creatures crowned with color call to her again. "Ground Dweller! Climb!" Even so, she struggled to find the courage to leave her hiding place.

Tiptoe remembered. "Release your fear, little one."

She forced herself into the sunlight and made the challenging climb to the porch. The screen and the back door were both wide open. Although she could not see the woman, she sensed she was not far away. Tiptoe stood at the entrance for some time, uncertain what to do next. A mysterious world, totally foreign to her, lay beyond the threshold. She mewed insistently, hoping the woman would discover her.

Tiptoe remembered. "Love will guide you."

She pulled herself up to the threshold, paused there a moment, and took a leap of faith into the laundry room. Her doubts totally vanished. She courageously followed the source of the sounds into the kitchen. "I know she is here. I know it!"

As Tiptoe scanned the large room, she nearly collapsed from happiness. She discovered her mother, lying comfortably on the inside of a fleece-lined jacket, placed on a stack of towels and newspapers to insulate it from the linoleum. Tiptoe forgot about the woman and her brothers waiting outside. She rushed toward her mother, mewing joyfully.

"Oh, Mother, where have you been? What happened to you?" Tiptoe panicked when she did not get an immediate response. "Mother!"

Geraldine opened her eyes and lifted her head. She was still too weak to do much more. "I am recovering, little one. I will regain my strength."

"Mother, you must recover!" Tiptoe was devastated. She had never seen her mother incapacitated.

"I have learned, my love, that there are some things beyond our control—yet all things are possible—if we accept the possibility." Geraldine suddenly noticed that two of her kittens were missing. "Tiptoe, where are . . ." she laid back again too weak to finish her thought.

"Don't worry, Mother. They are waiting outside. I will go get them."

As Tiptoe turned to leave her mother's side, she realized the woman was blocking her path. She considered making a run for the back door. Instead, she walked straight up to the woman, mewed softly, and rubbed against her ankles. The woman knelt down on one knee, stroked Tiptoe affectionately, and placed her on folded blankets next to her mother's bed. She petted them both gently and rose to walk toward the laundry room.

Tiptoe was frantic. She sensed the woman might close the back door and inadvertently separate her from Beetle and Whisper. She bolted through the kitchen, sliding across the linoleum as she turned the corner toward the open door. Her sudden dash for freedom startled the woman. She called to Tiptoe urgently. Tiptoe half climbed, half tumbled down the back stairs to the patio, and hid in a patch of ivy growing near the stairs. The woman did not pursue her. She also did not close the back door.

Tiptoe waited until she felt safe leaving the protection of the ivy and began the strenuous climb to the upper patio. She called to Whisper as she panted and struggled up the last two steps.

"Whisper! Whisper! Mother is in the human's den."

Whisper was astonished. He rushed to his sister, filled with pride for her courage and tenacity. "You saw her?"

"She is not her normal self. The human is helping her to recover. We must go to her before the final sound."

Whisper agreed.

"I was too excited to eat but I saw food for us and a warm sleeping place beside Mother. The human will accept us. I just know it."

"We will join Mother whatever the consequences. Now we must convince Beetle."

However, Beetle was about to realize his dream of freedom. He refused to enter the human's den for any reason and risk confinement.

"Consider this, brother. Where there is a way in, there is a way out. Come with us just until Mother is better. Then, do what you will. I am returning with Tiptoe."

Beetle would not follow. He was determined to snatch this opportunity to be free. He turned his back on his past, ran to the rear of the hill, and slipped through the broken slat in the fence into a new life of promise and adventure.

Whisper and Tiptoe waited for Beetle at the bottom of the stairs, hoping he would return.

"Do you feel he has left us?" Whisper asked sadly.

"Yes and no," answered Tiptoe.

Whisper felt reassured. "I know he loves Mother. I know he loves us."

"But he always *wants*."

"Mother taught us to understand the difference between what we want and what we need."

"And, he always wants more. Sometimes, more becomes too much." Tiptoe watched the back door anxiously. "What if we hear the final sound?"

"Then, we will go back to the den and return tomorrow. We will see the human again."

"Mother might worry if I don't return."

Whisper consoled her, "Mother will know what has happened. She always does."

"Yes," Tiptoe agreed. "That's true. But she is not herself now. Aren't you hungry . . . and thirsty?" She recalled the food waiting inside. "If we return to the den, what will we eat?"

Whisper considered the problem. He always looked forward to his next meal. He drew closer to his sister. "We'll find something to eat."

Whisper and Tiptoe kept their patient vigil at the bottom of the stairs. It was getting dark. The kittens understood it was too dangerous to wait much longer. Tiptoe focused her attention on the back porch. Both doors were still open. Whisper watched for Beetle. They huddled together to protect each other from the increasing cold, determined to wait until the last possible moment. Whisper could not hide his misgivings from his sister.

"It's time to go, isn't it," she stated with a grieving heart.

"Yes. Beetle has made his decision."

"I feel we will see him again."

"Maybe, one day."

"I will miss him."

"Me, too."

As Tiptoe and Whisper resigned themselves to necessity, they impulsively looked into each other's eyes and received the same mental picture. Beetle was coming down the hill! They climbed the stairs with the ease of pure joy to meet him on the patio, circling him, sniffing the fresh scent on his coat, brushing against him affectionately, demonstrating in every way possible how happy they were to be together again.

"Enough!" Beetle complained. "I couldn't leave—not like this. I'm smart enough to escape the human's control when the time comes."

The three kittens scampered to the threshold separating them from their mother.

"Wait!" Beetle ordered. "Who goes first?"

"Does it matter?" asked Whisper. "We can all greet Mother at the same time."

"The human has never seen either of you. You both must enter first," Tiptoe answered.

Beetle immediately jumped ahead, followed by his brother and his sister.

"Tiptoe, call to the human," he commanded. "I want her to know we are coming."

"Are you sure?"

"Absolutely."

Chapter 34

The woman was rinsing dishes at the kitchen sink. She heard the tiny mewing sound and knew the kitten had returned. She called back softly, stood perfectly still, and kept watch out of the corner of her eye. She was surprised to see a robust, black kitten with a few touches of white appear in the doorway to the kitchen, followed by an equally hearty white and black, and finally by the kitten she recognized. The white and black kitten stirred her memory. She did not pinpoint the reason at that moment.

"Well," she wondered. "How many of you are there?" She questioned what she would do with a houseful of cats. Fortunately, she had seen information at the clinic about organizations that would help her find homes for them at the appropriate time. She did not suspect the kittens might have their own ideas about the future.

The woman turned slowly from the kitchen sink to get a full view of the scene unfolding before her. She was uncertain whether the presence of the kittens would encourage or hinder the mother cat's recovery. They greeted their mother with affection and enthusiasm, but with a visible awareness of her fragility. They finally left her side to devour the food they seemed to know had been placed there for them. The woman added two more dishes to accommodate her unexpected guests.

As soon as the kittens finished eating, they examined every inch of the kitchen and laundry room. The smallest kitten discovered the litter pan and immediately discerned its purpose. The other two observed their littermate with interest as it scratched the sand zestfully and made use of it.

The woman had closed the door leading from the kitchen to the rest of the house. The back door and the screen were still wide open. She resisted the urge to try and prevent an escape. However, the kittens showed no interest in leaving. Once they had completed their thorough examination of the two rooms, they felt comfortable enough to play with one another for a short while and curl up together on the blankets to rest.

The woman locked the screen and the back door as quietly as possible and returned to the kitchen. She sat on the floor, observing the stray and her kittens, making a mental note of the supplies she would need in the future. As she reached over and, ever so gently, stroked the mother's head and neck, she recalled a dream that remained fresh in her mind. "I think I will call you, Geraldine." The stray opened her eyes and looked toward her for a split second. "Was that a response?" she asked herself whimsically.

The woman noticed the white and black kitten was sound asleep. On the other hand, she felt the smallest kitten observing her with an unsettling intelligence. The kitten pulled its paws to its chest and shifted its body, exposing a full, round belly, inviting her to pet it also. The black kitten rested with its head on its front paws, studying her with a mixture of curiosity and suspicion.

"What are you two thinking?" the woman asked aloud. She quickly admonished herself, "Cats don't think." She scratched the small kitten's belly softly. It remained on its back, twisting back and forth, suggesting she should continue. "Or do you?" she asked playfully as she obliged the kitten, rubbing its stomach in a gentle, circular motion. The sound of the doorbell changed her focus. The woman left the kitchen, curious about her unexpected caller.

Beetle sensed the identity of the visitor immediately. "It's him! The human . . . the one who doesn't like felines!"

Whisper and Tiptoe instinctively climbed into their mother's bed and lay as close as possible to her for protection. However, Whisper suddenly realized that for the first time since his birth his mother could not defend him. He composed himself, sat up straight, stretching to his full height, and asked gravely, "Why is he here?"

"Has he come for us?" Tiptoe asked fearfully.

Beetle ran toward the laundry room. "You can't trust humans. I tried to tell him this would happen."

"Who?" asked Tiptoe.

"Never mind! We have to get out of here."

Geraldine could still find the strength to mother her kittens. "Quiet yourselves, little ones." She strained to raise the upper half of her body. "You are feline. Make use of your unique abilities."

Tiptoe could feel the extent of her mother's weakness. Her large eyes begged forgiveness. "Mother, please lie back. We are old enough now to take care of ourselves." She added sheepishly, "We know better."

Whisper nuzzled his mother tenderly. "We just forgot."

Geraldine understood. "Yes, my loves. Sometimes, we forget."

Tiptoe and Whisper calmed themselves and waited for guidance. Beetle continued his frantic search for a way to escape.

"Listen to Mother," Tiptoe pleaded gently. "We are protected. Besides, I don't feel the visitor is hostile."

"He's not," Whisper agreed, "but our human certainly is."

Beetle stopped his search to focus his attention.

The woman opened the front door and automatically prepared for a confrontation. A neighbor with whom she had a disagreement stood before her with a large, black garbage bag at his side. She experienced a twinge of anger as she accepted the mysterious contents of the bag. She speculated how he would react if she informed him she was harboring the cat that had sparked their conflict—and her three kittens—in the kitchen. A sneaky suspicion that he knew increased her irritation.

The woman soon learned that her neighbor wanted to settle their differences. When she peeked inside the bag she found the courage to open her heart. His peace offering included a box of cat sand, a large cat pan, and a huge bag of kitten food. They both accepted the wisdom of compromise and declared a truce.

As the woman made a place in the laundry room for the supplies her neighbor had provided, she re-examined their conflict from a new perspective. She had always loved nature's beautiful landscapes and delightful creatures. She was able to forgive and forget its more savage aspects. However, the ancient precept to love your neighbor had proved more difficult. Forgive and forget was uphill work. She admitted to herself how often she had noticed the "speck" in her neighbor's eye and ignored the "plank" in her own. She was ready to look deeper and own her part in creating and sustaining the conflict.

A tiny shift in awareness cleared the way for positive change in their relationship.

The woman returned to the kitchen full of optimism. The events of that day had fallen into place with remarkable ease. She had considered her relationship with her neighbor beyond repair. Yet he had chosen this particular afternoon to settle their dispute and present his timely gifts. The mother cat and her kittens were resting together in a safe place. They had accepted a human presence and adapted quickly to a totally strange environment.

The mother cat seemed to be improving. The vet had pumped her full of fluids and antibiotics. The woman assumed the task of continuing the antibiotics and keeping her nourished and hydrated with a dropper, if necessary. She also assumed responsibility for administering mega-doses of love, the vet's highly recommended prescription for miracles. Was she witnessing a miracle? The woman thought so. She wondered how many other little miracles she had failed to notice in her life and promised herself to pay attention and to appreciate. The woman smiled and tiptoed from the laundry room at peace with life.

The kitchen door shut, and Beetle jumped to his feet.

"Lay down!" demanded Whisper. "We must be quiet so that Mother can rest."

Tiptoe now fully realized the seriousness of her mother's condition. "We must do everything we can to help her recover."

Beetle astonished both of them and reclined immediately. His mother was far more important to him than he chose to admit.

"Well, what do you think now?" Whisper asked his brother.

"About what?"

"Our human."

"We may be able to teach her a few things."

Whisper scowled at his brother. "Maybe we will learn something too!" He was impressed by his surroundings. He felt completely at ease with the human, good food a forearm's length away, and a soft, warm bed.

The kittens curled up close to one another, each absorbed in their own feelings about this new experience.

Tiptoe looked at Beetle thoughtfully. "Why did you decide to come back?"

Beetle avoided her glance, defending a story he did not wish to tell. "Go to sleep. I'm tired."

Tiptoe turned to Whisper, seeking his support. However, he was asleep again.

"Beetle, tell me why."

"I'm tired now. Ask me later."

Tiptoe rested her head on her front paws. "Oh, all right."

The image of a splendid white and black feline with gold, slanted eyes rimmed in black, and gorgeous white brows and whiskers passed through Tiptoe's mind. Her entire body tingled with excitement. She knew what had happened. However, she honored her brother and kept his secret.

Other Inspirational Books from Purple Haze Press Publisher

You Are What You Love©
By Vaishāli

You Are What You Love is the definitive 21st century guide for Spiritual seekers of timeless wisdom who have hit a pothole on the way to enlightenment and are searching for the answers to the big questions in life: "Who am I?" and "Why am I here?" Author Vaishāli explores mystic Emanuel Swedenborg's philosophy of gratitude and love. She expands this wisdom by associating it to traditional sources including Christianity and Buddhism. Through storytelling and humor, the focal point of the book "you don't have love, you are love" is revealed. A compelling read to deepen your understanding of Oneness.

Paperback, 400 pages, ISBN 978-0-9773200-0-4, $24.95

Also available on CD an 80-minute
condensed and abridged version of the 400-page book counter part.
Read by the author.
CD, ISBN 978-0-9773200-2-8, $14.95

Also available on CD an 80-minute condensed and abridged version of the 400-page book counter part. Read by the author.

CD, ISBN 978-0-9773200-2-8, $14.95

You Are What You Love Playbook
By Vaishāli

You Are What You Love Playbook is a playtime manual offering practical play practices to invoke play into action. Included is step-by-step guidance on dream work, a 13-month course in how to practice playful miracles, and a copy of the author's lucid dream diary. The perfect companion to You Are What You Love.

Paperback, 124 pages, ISBN 978-0-9773200-1-1, $14.95

Other Inspirational Books from Purple Haze Press Publisher

Wisdom Rising
By Vaishāli
Sometimes wisdom is best served up like M&M candies, in small pieces that you can savor, enjoy and hold in your hand. So it is with Vaishali's new book, "Wisdom Rising." It is a delightful, sweet, and satisfying collection of brilliant articles and short stories, that like gem quality jewels, are a thing of beauty, and a joy to behold.

It doesn't matter what your background is there is something to appeal to everyone in this book. Vaishali's trademark "out of the box" sense of humor and wild woman perspective runs rampant throughout the book. Whether she is talking about the Nature of God or simply poking fun at our own cultural insecurities and hypocrisies, Vaishali raises the bar on laugh out loud Spiritual wisdom. The entertainment as well as the wisdom rises flawlessly together, inviting the reader to go deeper in examining and showing up for their own life.

Everything about this book from the cover to the cartoon illustrations that punctuate every story, screams playful, fun, witty, and what we have seen Vaishali dish up before . . . which is the unexpected . . . no wonder she is know as "the Spiritual Wild Child."

Paperback, ISBN: 9773200-6-6 $14.95

Wisdom Rising, Book on CD
By Vaishāli
This 4-CD set is the condensed and abridged version of the 285 page book counter part. Read by the author.

CD, ISBN 987-0-9773200-9-7 $19.95

Other Inspirational Books from Purple Haze Press Publisher

LONGINUS: BOOK I OF THE MERLIN FACTOR
by Steven Maines

Longinus follows the tale of Gauis Cassius Longinus, the Roman Centurion who pierced the side Jesus with his spear while the condemned one hung from the cross.

After that fateful day, Longinus escapes Rome and the priests who want to take the spear and its supposed power for themselves. LONGINUS follows the Centurion's life from his love for the prostitute Irena to his mystical studies with the Druids of Gaul. But it also reveals Longinus' profound spiritual awakening through his Druidic studies and the spear that speaks to him with the voice of Christ.

Paperback, 241 pages, ISBN 978-0-9773200-3-5, $14.95

This abridged audio version of the critically acclaimed novel, LONGINUS: BOOK I OF THE MERLIN FACTOR by Steven Maines, follows the tale of Gauis Cassius Longinus, the Roman Centurion who pierced the side of Jesus with his spear while the condemned one hung from the cross. Abridged Audio Book (3 CD). As Read By Mark Colson

CD, ISBN 978-0-9773200-7-3, $19.95

MYRRIDDIN: BOOK II OF THE MERLIN FACTOR
by Steven Maines

In *MYRRIDDIN: Book II Of The Merlin Factor*, it is the 4th Century A.D. A young boy has found sacred relics of the early Christians in the ruins of an ancient Druid temple on the Isle Of Mystery in Old Britain. For reasons beyond his immediate comprehension, the lad connects with one item in particular; the Spear Of Longinus, the very spear that pierced the side of Jesus and allegedly holds the power of Christ. The boy's name is Myrriddin. The world would remember him as Merlin, the greatest Druid and Wizard of all time.

Paperback, 217 pages, ISBN 978-0-9773200-4-2, $14.95